THE EUROPEAN NOVELISTS SERIES

Edited by Herbert Van Thal

CHARLES DICKENS

CHARLES DICKENS

JULIAN SYMONS

ARTHUR BARKER LIMITED

5 WINSLEY STREET LONDON WI

SBN 213 17884 2

Printed in Great Britain by
Lowe & Brydone (Printers) Ltd., London

CONTENTS

CHAPTER I

THE LIFE

WHEN Charles Dickens died in 1870 he had become a national possession. The fact was recognised immediately : and *The Times* discussed on the leader pages of three consecutive issues his achievement, and his symbolic position in English life. *The Times'* first leader on 10th June 1870, the day after Dickens's death, began :

> Statesmen, men of science, philanthropists, the acknowledged benefactors of their race might pass away, and yet not leave the void which will be caused by the death of Dickens.

An article which appeared on the next day called the novelist a " great apostle of the people " and said that " His great characters have struck fast root in the hearts of his countrymen, for this, above all other reasons, that they are natural. . . . Every day will only add to the universal feeling that he wrote not for this age alone, but for all time."

Twelfth June was a Sunday, but on the 13th another first leader discussed Dickens ; the week-end had given Britain's national newspaper an opportunity to reflect on the proper resting-place of Britain's national novelist. " In the quiet hours of yesterday," it began, " many a thought will have turned to the great author who was with us a week ago, and who has passed so suddenly into those silent realms of which Sunday speaks to us." The writer went on to stress that, even though Dickens had expressed a wish to be buried at his home near Gad's Hill, and even though a public funeral was impossible because he had strictly forbidden it, the novelist could rest fittingly only in Westminster Abbey. "National grief feels that it owes national honours to the dead." This ukase was obeyed. Dickens was buried in the Abbey. The grave was kept open for two days so that the crowds of mourners could see the body; but they continued to come after it was closed, and Doctor Stanley, who delivered the funeral discourse on the following Sunday observed that "All day long there was a constant pressure to the spot, and many flowers were strewn upon it by unknown hands, many tears shed from unknown eyes."

There is no more dangerous omen for a writer's posthumous fame than the kind of canonisation given by Victorian public opinion to Dickens; for it made necessary an emphasis on the moral and sentimental aspects of his work, and a disregard of certain facets in his life and character which, taken together, have produced a positively false view of his career and achievement. When, in this century, the canonical veil was drawn gradually aside and it was revealed that Dickens probably behaved badly to his wife, and certainly had a young mistress who bore him an illegitimate child, the discovery affected drastically the critical view of his works as well as of his life. The Victorian Dickens, an amiable mixture of Santa Claus and his own Mark Tapley, is still celebrated by the Dickens Society and its curious publication, *The Dickensian*; while his modern detractors, with a simplicity equal to that of his Victorian admirers, have compared the views expressed by Dickens as a novelist with his actions as a man, and convicted him of hypocrisy. But it is irrelevant to make a moral case against Dickens which balances the moral case the Victorians made in his favour. The picture of him which has importance for us must relate his character to the discoveries of modern psychology, and his work to the social atmosphere and development of his own age. It must consider first his remarkable temperament, and its effect upon his writing ; and then the workings of such a temperament in the artistic conditions of the nineteenth century in England.

Charles John Huffam Dickens was born at Portsea on 7th February 1812. His father, John Dickens, was a clerk in the Navy Pay Office, an amiable, irresponsible, dandyish figure, who found it difficult to live on his salary of £350 a year without running into debt. In Charles's childhood the family moved from Portsea to London, from London to Chatham where Charles was sent to a day school, and from Chatham back to London. Their financial position worsened, and when Charles was twelve years old two events occurred within a month of each other which marked his character permanently. He was sent to work in a blacking warehouse, where he was paid 6s. a week ; and his father was arrested for debt, and lodged in the Marshalsea.

These two events both affected the course of Dickens's life : but in different ways. His father's imprisonment was a seed which bore a prolific literary growth ; it is reflected by Dickens's lifelong interest in prisons and the increasingly powerful descriptions of prison life in his books, from the articles on Newgate in *Sketches by Boz* to the recognisable portrait of John Dickens as Edward Dorrit, " father " of the Marshalsea. Dickens seems never to have felt it necessary to conceal the fact of his father's imprisonment, as many people, authors and others, would have done ; but the six months he spent working at Warren's Blacking

Factory caused him such anguish of mind that he never referred to them in conversation. His wife knew nothing of this time in his life, and his nearest approach to revealing it to any members of his family was when, in his last months, he was playing a Christmas game which involved remembering long strings of names contributed by each member of the company. When Dickens's turn came round he said, with " a strange inflection in his voice "— but with no attempt at explanation—" Warren's Blacking, 30 Strand." Similar hints of this childhood drudgery are to be found in his works, in casual asides about blacking warehouses which occur at odd times and places. But Dickens brought himself to write directly of this experience only once, in the fragment of autobiography which he set down at the age of thirty-five, and gave to his friend John Forster. In this fragment, later on adapted for use in *David Copperfield*, he tells of his misery at having to work " from morning to night, with common men and boys " at the task of covering pots of paste-blacking with a piece of oil-paper and then with a piece of blue paper, tying them round, clipping them neatly and labelling them. He does not complain of ill-treatment, but writes of his own " secret agony of soul " at being taken from school and sent to work with such ragged boys as Bob Fagin—whose surname he used afterwards in *Oliver Twist*. The words that Dickens uses in this recollection of his childhood show how painful the experience was to him. He says that he has no idea how long he worked at the blacking warehouse, " whether for a year, or much more, or less " (in fact it was six months). " That I suffered in secret, and that I suffered exquisitely, no one ever knew but I. How much I suffered it is, as I have said already, beyond any power to tell. No man's imagination can overstep the reality." The cup of his anguish was full when, while still working at the warehouse, he was taken to see his sister receive a prize for her musical studies.

The family fortunes improved, and the boy was taken from the warehouse and sent back to school. At the age of fifteen he began work as office boy to a solicitor, and then as a Law Courts reporter. When he was twenty years old he joined the staff of an evening paper named the *True Sun* as a Parliamentary reporter, and two years later went to the Whig *Morning Chronicle*, where he was not only Parliamentary reporter but was sent between sessions to report political speeches in various parts of the country ; and it was while he was working for the *Morning Chronicle* that he began to write the sketches of familiar scenes and characters that make up his first book. A pattern of frenetic excitement is noticeable in the young man's life and actions. It is typical that some of his shorthand notes should have been written " on the palm of my hand, by the light of a dark lantern, in a post-chaise and four, galloping through a wild country." It was his custom to work late at night on his sketches ; and he did so at times in spite of the fact that he suffered spasms of pain, which had affected him at intervals since childhood. These spasms had some of the characteristics of fits ; he had one of them at the blacking warehouse when he " rolled about on the floor " in " excruciating pain," while Bob Fagin filled empty blacking-bottles with hot water and held them to his side. In the days of his courtship of Catherine Hogarth, the colourless and amiable girl he married, Dickens wrote to her of dizziness affecting his sight, of " exquisite torture " or " an ecstasy of pain," to relieve which on one occasion he took a dose of henbane. But in spite of these spasms he was able to work with intense concentration for long periods of time. Nothing is more noticeable about his letters at this time to Catherine Hogarth than the frequency with which he apologised for not coming to see her because he was working feverishly. When she complained, he was curt :

> If the representations I have so often made to you, about my writing as a duty, and not as a pleasure, be not sufficient to keep you in good humour . . . why then, my dear, you must be out of temper, and there is no help for it.

It is at least possible that Dickens married the plump and placid Catherine Hogarth as a compensation for his rejection, three years earlier, by Maria Beadnell, the daughter of a bank manager. Dickens did everything possible to induce the Beadnell family, as well as Maria herself, to accept him as a suitor. He displayed versatility in the production of acrostics and poems for Maria's album, and wrote some hundreds of lines of rhymed verse which he called " The Bill of Fare," describing the good company to be found at the Beadnells' home. His suit was never warmly encouraged, however, and at last was rejected by the Beadnell family, it seems upon the ground that he was not socially eligible. Maria was sent to a finishing school in Paris, and Dickens was forbidden the Beadnell house. The letters he wrote secretly to Maria afford a startling contrast to the temperate correspondence he conducted with Catherine Hogarth. They contain no apologies for failure to keep appointments, nothing about " working as a duty " ; on the contrary, they express the writer's passion with overwhelming fervency. Dickens accuses Maria of heartless indifference, cruelty and coldness, and expresses himself as broken-hearted ; and although he received little encouragement, he did not break off the correspondence until it was absolutely plain that Maria had no intention of becoming the wife of a newspaper reporter.

The establishment set up by Dickens after his marriage was a curious one. Catherine's sixteen-year-old sister Mary Hogarth came to live with them ; and Dickens adored this young girl in much the same way that he had adored Maria Beadnell. When Catherine was expecting her first child, Mary Hogarth accompanied Dickens when he paid visits ; and her sudden death, which occurred a few months after she became a member of the Dickens household, was mourned by him as a lover. He took the ring from her finger and wore it on his own little finger until his death, and his prostration through grief was such that publication of *Pickwick*, which had begun in serial form, was interrupted for two months. John Forster, Dickens's friend and first biographer, says that Mary was " the ideal of his life," and it is obvious that his feeling for her was much more intense than the friendly affection he gave to his wife. It seems, also, that Dickens was able to feel intensely both for Maria Beadnell and Mary Hogarth to the degree that he could create them as ideal figures divorced in certain essential respects from reality.

Mary Hogarth remained an ideal because she died, so that Dickens was able to relive his suffering again and again by using her as a model for the perfectly pure, and exceedingly mortal, girls and women who appear in his novels. These characters had for him a reality which was in some ways almost greater than that of their originals. Thus he wrote to Forster, when planning the death of Little Nell in *The Old Curiosity Shop* :

> Nobody will miss her like I shall. It is such a very painful thing to me that I cannot really express my sorrow. Old wounds bleed afresh when I only think of the way of doing it : what the actual doing it will be, God knows.

Maria Beadnell, alive and married to somebody else, was a less satisfactory surrogate, and became less satisfactory still when, as Maria Winter, fat and garrulous, she renewed their acquaintance after a silence of more than twenty years. Dickens at first accepted her suggestion of a meeting with enthusiasm, but after it had taken place he found it convenient to avoid further encounters by reference to the restlessness and waywardness of an author's mind, and his devotion to art. Maria Beadnell had been the model for Dora in *David Copperfield* ; after meeting Maria Winter Dickens compensated himself by reproducing his own idealism and disillusionment through the relationship of Arthur Clennam and the stout, amiable, boring Flora Finching in *Our Mutual Friend*.

Dickens was from the beginning a remarkably successful author. The *Sketches by Boz* were a considerable success and *Pickwick Papers* made him a nationally famous figure at the age of twenty-five. During the three years after *Pickwick's* publication he earned £9,000, a large sum for a young writer even to-day, and at that time a considerable fortune ; it is remarkable that during this period he rarely had more than £100 in the bank. During the whole of his life Dickens earned enormous sums of money, yet he was never free from an eagerness to earn that led him to make contracts for books which could only be written within the stipulated time by prodigious exertion, and to quarrel with almost every publisher who produced his work. It is true that in these years his wife bore a great many children, and that he answered with unfailing generosity the many calls made upon him by other relatives ; but it is obviously inadequate to say, as does Bernard Shaw, that " he was forced to work himself to death prematurely to provide for them and for the well-to-do life he led." Other writers,

early manhood of an ability to exercise power over the minds of many of his friends. As a young man he was remarkably handsome, but this power was something more than the influence commonly exerted by those who are young, handsome and enthusiastic over those who lack all of those attributes : how much more Dickens discovered when, during his trip to America in 1842, he made casually an experiment on his wife which sent her into " magnetic sleep " in little more than two minutes. He became interested in the exercise of this hypnotic power, and began to use it with assurance ; his daughter Mamie says in her memoir of her father that she knows many cases, her own included, in which he used hypnosis with perfect success. On one occasion he " fell to " in the middle of the night, and " after a very fatiguing bout of it," put the artist John Leech into hypnotic sleep when he was suffering from congestion of the brain.

The most remarkable exercise of these hypnotic powers was in the case of Mrs. de la Rue, who met the Dickens family when they were travelling in Italy. Mrs. de la Rue, the wife of a Swiss banker, said that she was haunted by phantoms with veiled faces ; and Dickens hypnotised her once or twice a day in the attempt to dispel these fancies. When Dickens left Genoa he gave her " absent treatment " and in Naples was so anxious to have news of her state of health that he watched the arrival of the mail-bags into port through a telescope. The de la Rues rejoined Dickens and his wife, and to Catherine Dickens's distress the hypnotic sessions began again. On one occasion Dickens was wakened by Mr. de la Rue in the middle of the night and found the banker's wife rolled up into a ball, that could be unwound only by strokings and hypnotic passes. The sessions ended only when Catherine Dickens plainly showed jealousy, and ceased to be on speaking terms with the de la Rues.

This hypnotic power was closely associated with Dickens's love of acting. From earliest childhood he had both written and taken part in playlets, operettas and magic lantern shows. His first literary work, composed before he was ten years old, was a tragedy founded on one of the *Tales of the Genii*, called " Misnar, the Sultan of India " ; and the child was such an accomplished singer and actor that he was frequently placed on chairs or tables to display his talents in front of company. He thought of becoming an actor, and at the age of twenty was given an appointment for an audition before Charles Kemble ; but on the day he had a bad cold and inflammation of the face, and wrote postponing his attendance until the following season. He made no further attempt to go on the stage professionally, but his interest in it remained constant ; and friends remarked that he had the faculty, common to actors, of appearing continually to change his personality. Amateur theatricals were one of the chief pleasures and occupations of his later life. He spent much time and trouble in inducing such friends as Forster, Wilkie Collins, Douglas Jerrold and Mark Lemon to take part in them ; he was frequently stage manager of the plays presented, as well as a leading actor ; and these plays were almost always highly successful. It was this consciousness of hypnotic power and acting ability that made him turn in 1857, at one of the climacterics of his life, to the idea of giving public readings from his own works.

There can be detected in Dickens's letters and actions a deep consciousness of personal unfulfilment, and a flagging in his high animal spirits, after the publication of *David Copperfield* in 1850. It was during the same year that he started *Household Words* and took upon himself the full

burden of editorship, although four years earlier he had
abandoned editorship of the *Daily News* within three weeks
of the appearance of the first issue, after spending months
in gathering contributors together and learning exactly how
to run a newspaper. He had quarrelled with Bradbury, one
of the proprietors, about the extent of his editorial powers, yet
this does not seem an adequate explanation for his alternate
enthusiasm and indifference, and his hurried departure. If his
abandonment of the *Daily News* is contrasted with the energy
he displayed in relation to *Household Words*, it seems likely that
what Dickens really wanted was a vehicle for the expression
of his own feelings about life, and that a magazine was much
better suited to this purpose than a newspaper. Even though
he had to forget the idea of calling the paper by his own name,
and that of talking to his public through an omnipresent
Shadow, he was still able to make direct touch through *Household Words* with an audience to which he felt a personal relationship; and when in 1858 he separated from his wife he felt
it necessary to take the extraordinary step of printing a
statement in the magazine which appeared on the front
page, headed " Personal."

The idea of making such a statement was extremely
foolish : what is more interesting, however, is its revelation
of Dickens's state of mind in relation to his public. Certain
passages in the " Address " are particularly illuminating in
this respect :

> Three-and-twenty years have passed since I entered on my
> present relations with the public. . . . Through all that time
> I have tried to be as faithful to the public as they have been
> to me. It was my duty never to trifle with them, or deceive
> them, or presume upon their favour, or do anything with it
> but work hard to justify it. I have always endeavoured to
> discharge that duty.

My conspicuous position has often made me the subject of fabulous stories and unaccountable statements. Occasionally, such things have chafed me, or even wounded me ; but, I have always accepted them as the shadows inseparable from the light of my notoriety and success. I have never obtruded any such personal uneasiness of mine upon the generous aggregate of my audience. . . .

Some domestic trouble of mine, of long-standing, on which I will make no further remark than that it claims to be respected, as being of a sacredly private nature, has lately been brought to an arrangement. . . . By some means, arising out of wickedness, or out of folly, or out of inconceivable wild chance, or out of all three, this trouble has been made the occasion of misrepresentations, most grossly false, most monstrous and most cruel—involving, not only me, but innocent persons dear to my heart. . . .

The immediate, and nardly innocent, cause of the separation was a young actress named Ellen Lawless Ternan, who had become Dickens's mistress. There is some indication that on her side the alliance was made unwillingly, as a result of the pursuit of her pressed relentlessly by this famous man. On Dickens's side this love affair was yet another affirmation of the attraction that youth and childishness held for him (when Dickens first saw Ellen Ternan she was only eighteen years old, and was weeping because she had to appear on the stage showing her legs) ; but it was also an unsuccessful attempt to offset his discontent at the approach of middle age.

Dickens aged rapidly, as his photographs show ; and as he grew older he felt more and more lonely and, with no obvious reason, dissatisfied. " Why is it," he wrote to Forster in 1855, " That . . . a sense comes always crowding on me now, when I fall into low spirits, as of one happiness I have missed in life, and one friend and companion I have never made ? " This " one friend and companion," so far as she can be apprehended rationally, was the ideal woman prefigured by Dickens in later life as the dead Mary Hogarth and the married Maria Beadnell. He found two substitutes for these ideal figures of his recollection—Mary's sister Georgina, who became a member of the Dickens household, lived in it for many years, and took Dickens's side when he was separated from his wife ; and Ellen Ternan. But no living woman could be an adequate compensation for his ideal fantasy creation, and Dickens dramatised himself as a lonely figure at a time when he had an immense number of friends ; and he sought in the relationship with his " public " an intimacy that he had never been able to reach in private life. " I have no relief now but in action," he wrote to Forster in 1857. " I am become incapable of rest. I am quite confident that I should rust, break, and die, if I spared myself."

The public readings on which he embarked in 1858, the year of separation from his wife, fulfilled his need for action and travel ; they provided one more step in the relationship with his public which compensated for his failure in private life ; and they fulfilled, as nothing else but criminal activity could have done, his urgent need for emotional exhibitionism. Dickens continued the readings, with some intervals, until the end of his life, against the advice of many friends who considered them damaging both to his reputation and his health. They very largely took the place of writing as a creative activity. In the last twelve years of his life he completed only three novels.

The readings consisted of excerpts from his own works and stories, dramatised to gain the maximum emotional effect. They were extraordinary performances. Dickens acted all the parts in turn with remarkable vigour and passion, using falsetto voices for the women, and it has been suggested that the amazing effect he produced on audiences was attributable in part to his hypnotic power. He dressed with the greatest care for the readings, and in Ireland women gathered up the petals falling from his red geranium buttonhole, and begged for the stalk as a souvenir. In Dublin people paid £5 for a stall, and in Belfast at a *Dombey and Son* reading one man cried at the death of Paul, and another found Toots so ludicrous that he could not restrain his laughter. In Glasgow the tickets were oversold in error, dresses were torn, and the readings were made with people lying down upon the platform. Dickens was particularly pleased to find that he obtained " that peculiar personal relation between my audience and myself on which I counted most when I entered on this enterprise." The readings imposed great strain on him, mentally and physically, but he insisted on giving a second series, and then a third, although he felt some kind of deadness in his left side, and was unable to sleep. He undertook a series of readings in America and these too were enormously successful ; he worked throughout the tour in a state of almost continuous excitement, and lived on a daily diet made up of stimulants (a tumbler of cream with two tablespoonfuls of rum before rising, a pint of champagne at three) and sedatives (a frequent dose of laudanum at night).

It is impossible to read any account of these activities without realising that they were pathological in origin : that through them Dickens tried to release feelings of isolation, terror and criminal passion that sprang from his childhood and had haunted him for years, and that the " peculiar personal relation " established with the audience was essentially that of a hypnotist and his patient. The culminating point of the readings was one from *Oliver Twist*, showing the murder of Nancy by Sikes ; and although Dickens hesitated about including this reading in his repertoire because it might be " so horrible as to keep them away another time," he finally decided in favour of its inclusion. Again his friends advised against it : but they were disregarded. The effect was all he had expected : at Clifton they had " a dozen to twenty young ladies taken out stiff and rigid." A friend wrote to him : " I am bound to tell you that I had an almost irresistible impulse upon me to *scream* and that if anyone had cried out I should have followed." The strain of acting the parts was enormous, and alarming symptoms of paralysis showed themselves. Dickens insisted, however, that the Sikes and Nancy reading should be continued. He became fascinated by it, and gave it again and again ; it had become, he told his manager, " a kind of novelty." The manager noticed that after performing this reading he would try to return to the stage, or give way to apparently involuntary bursts of laughter. At last his uncertainty of touch, movement and voice became so marked that the whole series of readings had to be given up.

Most of the year of life left to him was spent, fairly quietly, at his home at Gad's Hill. He recovered health sufficiently to speak at banquets ; he even carried through successfully another series of twelve readings, although Forster says that " hardly a day passed unvisited by some effect or other of the disastrous excitement " ; he began *Edwin Drood*. He had the impression always that the symptoms of paralysis which became every week more apparent were caused by something in the medicine he was given, and he never despaired of complete recovery ; there is little indication that, even in his last weeks of life, he realised that the flame which had burned in him so furiously was almost extinguished.

He began *Edwin Drood*, and worked on it with less than his old power of concentration, but more than his old care ; he replied to the toast of "Literature" at the Academy dinner ; in June he undertook the stage management of private theatricals in which his children Mamie and Kate played parts. On the day of these theatricals he made his will, in which the first bequest was a sum of £1000 to Ellen Ternan. Six days later, when he sat down to dinner, after a day spent in his garden chalet working on *Edwin Drood*, he told Georgina Hogarth that for an hour he had been very ill. He rose from the table, and would have fallen but for her support. She tried to get him to the sofa and he said "On the ground." Those were the last coherent words he spoke.

"They charm us by their intellectual mobility, their versatility, their wealth of ideas, their ready accessibility and their delight in adventure, their artistic capacity, their good nature, their cheery, sunny mood. But at the same time they put us in an uncomfortable state of surprise by a certain restlessness, talkativeness, desultoriness in conversation, excessive need for social life, capricious temper and suggestibility, lack of reliability, steadiness, and perseverance in work, a tendency to building castles in the air and scheming, occasional unusual activities. Now and then one possibly hears also of periods of causeless depression or anxiety. . . ."

This remarkably apt description of Dickens is in fact a quotation from Professor Emil Kraepelin's book, *Manic-Depressive Insanity and Paranoia*. Professor Kraepelin is describing the slightest form of manic-depression which remains "still in the domain of the normal," and touches especially "brilliant, but unevenly gifted personalities with artistic inclinations." None of Dickens's biographers, as far as I know, has attempted to assess his personality in the terms of modern psychology ; as soon as one does so, it becomes obvious that he shows strongly marked manic-depressive traits, and that his peculiar psychological disposition had a strong effect upon his work.

Psychologists use the term *manic-depressive* for a type of mental illness which, although many of its symptoms vary from individual to individual, is marked always by rapid alternations of apparently causeless exultation (hypomania) and equally causeless depression. In extreme cases the manic-depressive suffers, during attacks, from fixed delusions : caricatures grin out of the book he wishes to read, worms swarm in his food, warning voices cry at him through windows. There are, however, many milder forms of the condition ; in them patients experience abnormal reactions to external stimuli. They lose for a time the mastery over their range of ideas ; they forget the simplest things, and cannot remember where they are. (As Dickens upon occasion lost all idea of his situation and condition.) Childhood experiences are often, in perfectly good faith, represented by them otherwise than as they actually occurred. (We remember that Dickens did not know whether he had spent months or years at the blacking warehouse.) The patient feels utterly alone, and indescribably unhappy ; as Dickens, surrounded by friends and at the height of his fame, lamented the " one friend and companion I have never made." These are characteristics of the depressive state : in mania the patient has ideas of greatness (Dickens referred to himself in letters, more in earnest than in jest, as the " Inimitable "). The feeling of fatigue, in mania, is completely absent, and the most intense excitement can be sustained for weeks, " perhaps because of the ease with which activity discharges itself" (Kraepelin) ; appetite is often increased, but becomes markedly irregular ; the patient feels the need of an extreme pressure of activity :

" As he is a stranger to fatigue, his activity goes on day and night ; work becomes very easy to him ; ideas flow to him. He cannot stay long in bed ; early in the morning, even at four o'clock, he gets up, he clears out lumber rooms, discharges business that was in arrears, undertakes morning walks, excursions. He begins to take part in social entertainments, to write many long letters. . . . He finds complete satisfaction in the enjoyment of friendship, of art, of humanity ; he will make everyone happy, abolish social wretchedness, convert all in his surroundings. For the most part an exuberant, unrestrained mood inclined to practical jokes of all kinds is developed." (Kraepelin.)

It is obvious that these are Dickens's characteristics ; and although it is true that some of them are shown by many people upon occasion, they mark Dickens persistently and strongly. If we are looking for the causes of his condition, it will certainly be relevant to remember that he was a delicate and excitable child, and that from an early age he was encouraged to dress up, and to play parts in theatricals. It would be interesting, also, to know much more than we are ever likely to learn about the mysterious fits or spasms which Dickens's biographers mention so casually. If they were epileptic in origin, they were probably a contributory cause of his tendency to manic-depression.

There is a school of nineteenth-century æsthetic critics which maintains that a man's psychology, and his private life, have nothing to do with his writings. In a sense they are quite right. It is possible to write about Dickens, or anybody else, simply in social terms, or in moral terms, or in technical literary terms ; but in the case of such a writer as Dickens, and in such an age as our own, such approaches are unsatisfactory, because they are incomplete. Any criticism of Dickens which is relevant for our time must recognise that he was not primarily a conscious literary artist like Jane Austen or Henry James : but a man obsessed. Before we can truly evaluate his work as artistic expression, we must realise that it was for Dickens first of all emotional expression produced by relentless psychological necessity. We can recognise, and to a certain degree we can separate, the conscious and unconscious elements in his work : the conscious element which belongs to the radical, the sentimentalist, the respectable bourgeois, the dandy, the " Inimitable " ; and the unconscious, irrational, almost wholly neurotic element that lies beneath it. In extreme forms manic-depression precludes the creation of art ; in a mild form it permits the existence of the split-artist, the man struggling to make a rational world from his own passionate, and apparently causeless, exaltation and depression : of Charles Dickens.

CHAPTER II

THE WORK

THE *Sketches by Boz* written by Dickens in his early twenties show already his absorption in the themes that were to occupy him as a writer. There is the interest in violence and in criminal action, which has a literary source in the Gothic novel, a psychological one in Dickens's own character and childhood experience, and a social one in the management of prisons and the condition of the working class at that time. The study of Newgate prison in this first book is an excellent piece of reporting on prison life, to which has been added an imaginative reconstruction of the last night of a man condemned to execution ; " The Drunkard's Death " describes a drunken father's betrayal of his son to the police, the drunkard's suicide, and the washing ashore of his body, " a swollen and disfigured mass " ; and " The Black Veil " tells the story of a man who has been hanged, and whose body has been obtained by his mother for revival by a doctor. There is the delight in descriptions of food which becomes an obsession in *Pickwick Papers*, is present to a less degree in most of the other early novels, and fades away (with Dickens's ebbing vitality ?) in the last books. There is the election for beadle between Bung and Spruggins which is a prefigurement of Eatanswill, and of the later and more savage pictures of all political activity as pure chicanery. There is the delight in the stagecoach and hackney coach as symbols of the good things in the existing order of society, as opposed to the railway train which represented for Dickens all the worst characteristics of utilitarianism. There is the distrust of professional philanthropy, shown in the portrait of the missionary, forebear of Mrs. Jellyby and Mrs. Pardiggle, who "repeated a dialogue he had heard between two negroes, behind a hedge, on the subject of Distribution Societies," to the sound of tumultuous applause.

Sketches by Boz is a book generally ignored, or touched on lightly, by Dickens's most enthusiastic admirers : but it is an important book, not only because it suggests many themes elaborated in the later work, but because it shows how, right at the outset of his career, Dickens's feelings were perfectly at one with those of his chosen audience. For the most remarkable thing about this collection of hastily written sketches is the extraordinary sense their author has of the values of his audience, the certainty of tone in which he writes notes on neighbourhood characters and the broker's man and the humours of the Tuggses at Ramsgate. The class for which Dickens wrote was the ascending bourgeoisie, and in conscious belief he adhered utterly to its scale of values. The lower class, in his work, are comic figures when well treated by their masters ; when badly treated by unjust masters they are pathetic. The aristocracy and upper class may be selfish or stupid, and very often they have a family secret to hide in the form of some blemish of birth or crime. The professional class are seen, with very few exceptions, as a parasitic growth upon the upper class. But the central characters of Dickens's novels, both heroes and villains, belong generally to the bourgeoisie. They are merchants and shopkeepers, near-gentlemen and white-collar office workers, young men with a position in society rendered dubious by the source, or the lack, of their income. In these first sketches can be seen plainly the separate strands that made up the body of

his work : the radical social strand, the comic and sentimental strand, the horrific strand. It is convenient to
consider them apart, although in fact they were often
interwoven : convenient, because in this way we can most
easily distinguish the contradictory elements in his very
complicated nature.

THE RADICAL

Dickens's radicalism is apparent throughout the whole
course of his writing. It is radicalism of a very curious
kind. He was opposed to the existing order of society, in
the sense that he saw injustices committed, laws administered
harshly, and all sorts of social miseries tacitly allowed to
exist : but he was not opposed to the existing order in the
sense of wishing to reform it through Parliament, or to
overthrow it by extra-Parliamentary means. Indeed, it can
hardly be said that, in a consciously political sense, Dickens
was a radical at all. We have seen already that he had no
patience with the workings of the Parliamentary system:
but it is important to realise that he had no capacity for
understanding the practical side of politics and government.
His years as a Parliamentary reporter allowed him to see
in Parliament only a solemnly obscene farce. Elections in
his novels are at once corrupt and comic, members of
Parliament are mere strutting boobies, and in *Bleak House*
the Parliamentary apparatus itself is ridiculed when Boodle,
Coodle and Doodle are presented as the political alternative
to Buffy, Cuffy and Duffy. But Dickens's criticism of
Parliamentary institutions and practice, like his criticism of
the Civil Service, was not based on intellectual understanding
and rational condemnation, but on moral feeling. Mr.
Shaw, in applauding Dickens as a revolutionary, says that

he had probably never heard of Marx : it would be more to the point to say that there is no sign in his novels, or I think in his correspondence, that he had ever read any serious economic or philosophical works, excepting those of Carlyle. His judgements of individual instances of cruelty and oppression were made in absolute ignorance of any general principles about the conduct of society. They were consistently moral : their morality was rooted in the childhood injustices he had suffered, and in his own uncertain position as one who at the height of his fame was regarded as a national, but not in the highest circles a social, asset.

Sketches by Boz contains hints of radical feeling in the London and parish sketches, and *Pickwick Papers* in the Parliamentary and prison scenes. In this book, too, Dickens first began to subject legal processes to a moral bombardment that was repeated, with variations, in more than half of his novels. It would be difficult to discover exactly what Dickens demanded of the law or of Parliament, and perhaps he did not know himself. He seems to have believed in his youth that with a little goodwill on the part of everybody lawyers would cease to defend guilty clients or barristers use rhetoric to secure the conviction of innocent ones. Goodwill, indeed, was Dickens's prescription at this time for the social ills he diagnosed ; the goodwill of officials could make the Poor Law work benignly, the goodwill of employers could provide reasonable living and working conditions for employees, the goodwill of rich, benevolent individuals could rescue the poor and the unhappy from degradation. Thus Mr. Pickwick, who had " far more than a man at my age can ever live to spend," was able to redeem the worthless Jingle and Job Trotter ; Mr. Brownlow, a rich, retired merchant, to hover like an elderly angel over the life of

Oliver Twist ; and the brothers Cheeryble, ideal employers who were always thinking of ways to please their staff, to solve all of Nicholas Nickleby's financial problems.

The books that follow *Pickwick* develop Dickens's individual radicalism, and draw freely upon his childhood memories of the blacking warehouse and of poverty. *Oliver Twist* tells the misadventures of a child born in a workhouse and thrown among thieves, receivers and murderers ; *Nicholas Nickleby* exposes through Dotheboys Hall and Wackford Squeers what the author called in his Preface " the monstrous neglect of education in England, and the disregard of it by the State as a means of forming good or bad citizens." Treatments of such subjects in such a tone was something new in literature, and the success of the books was based partly on the picture of " low life " in *Oliver Twist* and the storm raised by the exposure of private schools in *Nicholas Nickleby*. These were subjects, and this was an attitude that could be appreciated by the new reading class, the rising bourgeoisie whose power had been released by the Industrial Revolution and formally acknowledged in the Reform Act of 1832, the class that was to play a major part in developing British Imperialism abroad through ruthless exploitation, while trying at the same time to salve uneasy consciences with such minor measures of reform at home as Factory Acts that limited working hours to ten a day. Dickens was the conscience of this rising bourgeoisie, and he never moved outside the ethics of his class. It has been said that his attitude was that of a nineteenth-century liberal : but to say that is to do Dickens both more and less than justice, and to disregard his acute distaste for the liberal rationalism of his age. His sympathy for the oppressed was wholly emotional, and took the form of a drama in which he was the central figure.

" I mean to strike the heaviest blow in my power for these unfortunate creatures," he wrote in 1838 after he had seen the miserable lives of workers in cotton mills ; the emphasis, as always, is upon his individual influence and not upon any concerted plan. Thus, although he expressed a cautious sympathy for Chartism in its early days, and wrote to Forster in 1841, " By Jove, how radical I am getting," his real enthusiasm was given to helping Miss Burdett Coutts with schemes for ragged schools and slum clearance. Such activities were fully in keeping with his unwitting role as the conscience of the bourgeoisie.

It was in this capacity that he roused an emotion, remarkable even in Victorian times, by the pathetic and sentimental scenes in his early novels. When Forster read one of Dickens's Christmas stories, *The Chimes*, to a friend, " He cried so much, and so painfully, that Forster didn't know whether to go on or stop." After the death of Little Nell in *The Old Curiosity Shop*, a neighbour of Lord Jeffrey found him in tears. " I'm a great goose," he said, " to have given way so." Dickens's letters to his wife are full of references to friends crying, or being thrown " into a dreadful state " by readings from his books, and it is clear that such effects were for him a test of success. He produced the same effect in later life upon those who attended his public readings ; and it is notable that he had by then lost to some degree the capacity to obtain it directly through writing. The effect of the production of such work upon Dickens himself was equally remarkable. At the height of his excitement in writing *The Chimes* his face became white, his cheeks sunken, his hair lank. He felt hot and giddy. When the story was finished he was obliged to lock himself indoors because his face " was swollen for the time to twice its proper size."

When Dickens's position as a great novelist became firmly established, his radicalism changed. As a public man he interested himself in schemes for better housing, sanitary reform, the rescue of prostitutes ; he supported ardently the General Theatrical Fund Association for poor and invalid actors and actresses. He produced and acted in several plays to assist indigent writers like Leigh Hunt and Sheridan Knowles, and spent a great deal of time in work for the " Guild of Literature and Art," through which writers and artists were to be given houses in which they could live and work rent free. This scheme was begun in 1850, with the support of Dickens and Lytton, but when in 1865 the first three Guild houses were ready for occupation, it proved impossible to find anybody to come and live in them.

In literature his radicalism became at once more bitter, and less concerned with practical issues. The note of reforming zeal is apparent in all of the early novels, not only in the attacks on specific social evils, but in passages of moralising such as this one from *The Old Curiosity Shop* :

> Oh ! if those who rule the destinies of nations . . . would but think how hard it is for the very poor to have engendered in their hearts that love of home from which all domestic virtues spring, when they live in dense and squalid masses where social decency is lost, or rather never found—if they would but turn aside from the wide thoroughfares and great houses, and strive to improve the wretched dwellings in bye-ways where only Poverty may walk—many low roofs would, point more truly to the sky, than the loftiest steeple that now rears proudly up from the midst of guilt, and crime, and horrible disease, to mock them by its contrast.

The hopeful note of such a characteristic passage is based upon the belief, already mentioned, that reform could be effected by the action of benevolent rulers—the political counterparts of those rich merchants who solved the problems of so many of the characters in Dickens's own early books. Such a belief could hardly survive the experiences of the eighteen-forties—the brutal defeat of Chartism and the beginning of organised Trade Unionism in England, and in Europe the revolutions of 1848 with their repercussions on British politics and economy. Dickens could not preserve his belief in private benevolence as a cure for social evils, but neither could he look with favour on any organised movement of the working-class. *Barnaby Rudge* contains a savage caricature of early trade unionism in the picture of Sim Tappertit's " Prentice Knights " with their comic opera paraphernalia of thigh-bones and skulls ; and although the period of *Barnaby Rudge* is the late eighteenth century the book was actually written in 1840 and the attack clearly reflected Dickens's view of contemporary attempts to organise employees against employers. The only other picture of trade unionism in Dickens is found in *Hard Times* (1854), where Stephen Blackpool, the " good " worker, refuses to join the " United Aggregate Tribunal," which employs an agitator named Slackbridge to further its cause among the workers, " an ill-made, high-shouldered man, with lowering brows, and his features crushed into an habitually sour expression." But although Dickens disliked the organisation of workers into trade unions, he reserved his particular execration for that " creature of very mysterious existence," as he called it, " the mob." His hardly-won social position and his childhood experiences alike made Dickens distrustful of " the mob." It was, in one sense, " the mob " from which Dickens himself had escaped, or emerged, to take up a position in respectable bourgeois society ; in another aspect, " the mob " threatened the whole structure of that society and its scale of values ; and in another still, " the mob's " capacity for destruction fascinated Dickens in the same way that nihilism fascinated Russian intellectuals of the same period. The triumph of " the mob " signified for Dickens the release of the criminal elements in society. Something in him responded to such a prospect, as something in Dostoievsky and Turgenev reflected the nihilists they depicted.

There was, however, a contradiction in Dickens's treatment of " the mob," of which he must have been uncomfortably conscious. It resided in the anomalous fact that " the mob " was made up of the same poor and wretched men and women on whose behalf Dickens conducted many of his activities as a reformer. He avoided this contradiction by dealing with " the mob " as a historical, rather than a contemporary, entity. In his two historical novels, *Barnaby Rudge* (1841) and *A Tale of Two Cities* (1859), incomparably the most vivid scenes are those which deal with revolutionary violence. Dickens's conscious attitude towards this violence is one of unqualified horror : appalled by " the mob's " destructive activity, he does his best to deny that it is made up of men and women. In *Barnaby Rudge* this " creature " is like the ocean, fickle, uncertain, terrible when roused ; it rages and roars " like a mad monster " ; it is " a dream of demon heads and savage eyes " ; those in it wrench flowers from their stalks " like savages who twisted human necks." In *A Tale of Two Cities* the mob are " like demons," who have little relation to humanity. The faces of men at a grindstone " were more horrible and cruel than the visages of the wildest savages in their most barbarous disguise. False eyebrows and false moustaches were stuck upon them, and their hideous countenances were all bloody and sweaty, and all awry with howling, and all staring and glaring with beastly excitement and want of sleep." It has been remarked that such passages show Dickens's " horror of revolutionary hysteria," but they show much more clearly his own hysteria in face of violence, and his terror at the threat such violence offered to the very root of society. With the terror went fascination ; there is no more fully felt character in *Barnaby Rudge* than Dennis the hangman, who joins Lord George Gordon's conspiracy so that he will have opportunities to exercise his skill. When Dennis comes to see Gordon's secretary, Gashford, he insists that arrested Papists must be hanged. " I mustn't have no biling, no roasting, no frying—nothing but hanging." No scene in the book is more horrible or more ludicrous than that in which Dennis takes part in the attack on Newgate prison, and then tries to prevent four prisoners, who are due to be hanged on the following day, from being rescued by the rebels. Seen from one point of view Dennis, with his insistence on the legal propriety of his occupation, reflects simply a Jonsonian humour ; seen from another, he expresses the mingled fear and desire in Dickens himself that prompted his lifelong interest in hanging. In *A Tale of Two Cities* Madame Defarge with her knitting plays a similar part to that allotted to Dennis in the earlier book ; and although the guillotine and blood are the chief symbols of violence in this book, hanging is not ignored. The hanging of Foulon, who told the people that " they might eat grass " is described with hysterical excitement and passionate power :

> Down, and up, and head foremost on the steps of the building ; now, on his knees ; now, on his feet ; now, on his back . . . torn, bruised, panting, bleeding, yet always entreating and beseeching for mercy . . . he was hauled to the nearest street corner where one of the fatal lamps swung, and

there Madame Defarge let him go—as a cat might have done
to a mouse—and silently and composedly looked at him while
they made ready, and while he besought her : the women
passionately screeching at him all the time, and the men sternly
calling out to have him killed with grass in his mouth. Once,
he went aloft, and the rope broke, and they caught him
shrieking ; twice, he went aloft, and the rope broke, and they
caught him shrieking ; then, the rope was merciful, and held
him, and his head was soon upon a pike.

It is often said that many of the figures in Dickens's books
are caricatures. It would be nearer to the truth to say that
they are pathological distortions of human egoism, in which
a thwarted radical enacts forbidden scenes of violence
through the mouths and bodies of characters labelled *wicked*.
Even in *Pickwick Papers*, a book generally regarded as one
continuous roar of laughter, the stories-within-stories in the
book contain scenes such as that in " A Madman's Manuscript," in which the narrator tells of " the pleasure of
stropping the razor day after day, feeling the sharp edge,
and thinking of the gash one stroke of its thin bright edge
would make ! " Fagin (" like some loathsome reptile . . .
crawling forth, by night, in search of some rich offal for a
meal ") and Bill Sikes in *Oliver Twist* are certainly pathological cases ; and Dickens's interest in hanging is exploited
in this book through making Sikes hang himself by accident,
and in a lengthy description of Fagin's feelings at his trial.
Squeers and the moneylender Arthur Gride in *Nicholas
Nickleby*, Quilp in *The Old Curiosity Shop*, Major Bagstock
and Toots in *Dombey and Son*, are all figures who can be
viewed more satisfactorily in the light of pathology than
through any attempt to assess their actions rationally. Toots,
who writes letters to himself " from persons of distinction "
and preserves them in his desk, is characteristic of the minor
figures in the early and middle books whose eccentricity

stretches far beyond the limits of ordinary caricature. The only one of these grotesques drawn at full length is Quilp, the hunchbacked monster of evil in *The Old Curiosity Shop*. Quilp is one of the most extraordinary of Dickens's creations, and yet one of his least successful ; for, having created this monstrous machine, Dickens can find no adequate work for it to do. At breakfast Quilp eats eggs shell and all, devours gigantic prawns with their tails on, drinks boiling tea without winking and bites his fork and spoon until they bend. His aspect is normally that of a " panting dog," but he can change expression with great facility. Thus, when his mother-in-law shakes her fist at him in the glass, the mirror shows her " the reflection of a horribly grotesque and distorted face with the tongue lolling out," but in the next instant, when she turns round, Quilp faces her placidly and asks gently : " How are you now, my dear old darling ? "

Quilp's activities (partly because of the emphasis placed upon Little Nell, Dickens's first full triumph of pathetic sentiment) are confined to such minor unpleasantness as tormenting his wife and the boy who works at his wharf ; but there is a remarkable scene near the end of the book in which, burked in his zest for criminal activity, Quilp batters away at a great ship's figure-head in the wooden cabin on his wharf because he thinks it is like Kit Nubbles. After screwing gimlets into the figure and sticking forks into its eyes, Quilp beats at the great face, searing it with a red-hot poker. As a toast to these activities he raises a hot saucepan to his lips, and drinks up a half-pint of bubbling and hissing rum.

Quilp represents for Dickens the sinister side of radicalism, although he would not have identified it in that way. Dennis, Quilp and other figures in the early novels, have a pure urge for destruction : they are, for Dickens, a logical extension of the violence that must be involved in a radicalism which passed beyond the mild social reforms which he always saw himself effecting in person. In this sense only, the crude Marxist view of Dickens, expressed by Mr. T. A. Jackson, is acceptable. Mr. Jackson writes of Dickens's " growing sense that the only possible remedy " for social evils was " complete social revolution," which " seemed completely unattainable." No doubt Dickens thought social revolution unattainable : but the idea, implicit in Mr. Jackson's remarks, that he thought it desirable, is altogether incorrect. On the contrary, since Dickens viewed all social conflicts in personal terms, such a conclusion brought him sad disillusionment. In later life he could no longer think of social evils being remedied through the agency of a series of benevolent, measurelessly wealthy figures ; and where the problems of the heroes in his early books are solved simply through the amiability of the god in the counting house, Pip in *Great Expectations* and old Dorrit in the novel that bears his name, find happiness, as far as they find it at all, only when they are poor.

The social criticism in the later novels becomes increasingly bitter with Dickens's own growing disillusionment about the behaviour of human beings : he is no longer able even to suggest any cure for the corruption he exposes, yet his excoriation of this corruption and dishonesty has become more savage. *David Copperfield* (1850), Dickens's most plainly autobiographical novel, is the last book in which he is able to view with any optimism his own eventual position in society ; and even here the success story is artificially contrived, whereas David's miserable childhood and the sorrows of his manhood fully engage his creator's sympathy. David's success as an author is sketched so casually that we do not know any of the steps that took him to fame, nor are we told the name of one of his books. In this book Dickens is so little interested in the practical details of his hero's later career that he grants him success, and a happy marriage with Agnes Wickfield, as a mere formality. His interest is truly engaged, however, by David's emotional relations with Dora and Steerforth. When Dora (a blending of several women emotionally important to him) dies, Dickens ascribes to David his own growing feeling of life's meaninglessness:

> I came to think that the Future was walled up before me, that the energy and action of my life were at an end, that I never could find any refuge but in the grave. . . . From the accumulated sadness into which I fell, I had at length no hope of ever issuing again. I roamed from place to place, carrying my burden with me everywhere. I felt its whole weight now ; and I drooped beneath it, and I said in my heart that it could never be lightened.

This consciousness of defeat in what he conceived as a personal struggle with society colours darkly all of Dickens's last novels. In them he impales on the skewer of his own bitterness the bureaucracy that had rebuffed his work as a reformer, the aristocracy that had rejected him as a social equal, the friends and lovers who had failed to live in the fantasy-world of his creation. In *Bleak House* (1851), *Hard Times* (1854), *Little Dorrit* (1856), *Great Expectations* (1861) and *Our Mutual Friend* (1865) Dickens created a world like that of no other English novelist, in which the good characters are either fools or lunatics caught up in a vicious whirlpool that makes nonsense of their attempts at benevolence ; and the bad are bloodless embodiments of evil institutions, or reformers of a kind really not very different from Dickens himself, but with all their human weaknesses displayed under the largest of magnifying glasses. In *Bleak House* this class of " good " but eccentric characters is represented by Jarndyce, a pathetically ineffective copy of the omnipotent benefactors of the early novels, Boythorn, who spends his endless energy in a foolish legal action about a right-of-way, and an amiable elderly lunatic named Miss Flite. The organisation of social benevolence is caricatured in Mrs. Jellyby, who is active in arranging the betterment of the natives of Borrioboola-Gha but neglects her own family, and in a terrifying Victorian health visitor named Mrs. Pardiggle. The mechanism of legal bureaucracy is typified in three very different lawyers, Tulkinghorn, Vholes and Conversation Kenge. The decadence of the aristocracy is suggested in the description of the life led by Sir Leicester and Lady Dedlock, and even more by the glimpses we get of Lady Dedlock's " place " in Lincolnshire, Chesney Wold. Dickens's ability to convey social atmosphere through the description of houses and landscape is shown excellently here ; the first sight of Chesney Wold sets the tone for all the events that take place there :

> The waters are out in Lincolnshire. An arch of the bridge in the park has been sapped and sopped away. The adjacent low-lying ground, for half a mile in breadth, is a stagnant river, with melancholy trees for islands in it, and a surface punctured all over, all day long, with falling rain. My Lady Dedlock's " place " has been extremely dreary. The weather, for many a day and night, has been so wet, that the trees seem wet through, and the soft loppings and prunings of the woodman's axe can make no crash or crackle as they fall. The deer, looking soaked, leave quagmires where they pass. The shot of a rifle loses its sharpness in the moist air, and its smoke moves in a tardy little cloud towards the green rise, coppice-topped, that makes a background for the falling rain. The view from my Lady Dedlock's own windows is alternately a lead-coloured view, and a view in Indian ink. The vases on

the stone terrace in the foreground catch the rain all day ; and the heavy drops fall, drip, drip, drip, upon the broad flagged pavement, called, from old time, the Ghost's Walk, all night. On Sundays, the little church in the park is mouldy ; the oaken pulpit breaks out into a cold sweat ; and there is a general smell and taste as of the ancient Dedlocks in their graves.

The scene symbolises the decay of a class, and of a way of living ; and there is no adequate counter statement of the values of the rising forces in society. Mr. Jarndyce is willingly deceived by Skimpole ; the young, bright Richard Carstone, who would have been a successful lover in an earlier book, is eaten away like Miss Flite by the slow corrosion of the law ; and the happy ending awarded to Esther Summerson is out of keeping with the book's general tone.

Bleak House is primarily a study in decay. *Little Dorrit*, the next long novel, is a study in snobbery. The Circumlocution Office takes the place of the legal profession as a bureaucratic target, and a particular section of the new rich is derided for its attempt to infiltrate into the upper class. The study of snobbery takes place on several levels ; it is dealt with most comprehensively through the effect of good fortune on the Dorrit family. Old Mr. Dorrit is able to find ground for self-satisfaction and amiable condescension in his position as " father " of Marshalsea prison. Released, and placed unexpectedly in possession of a fortune, he turns from a sponger into a feeble tyrant, rebuffs the acquaintances to whom he had formerly condescended, and engages a superannuated model of propriety named Mrs. General, " a cool, waxy, blown-out woman, who had never lighted well," to complete the education of his daughters. Mr. Dorrit is a compound of Pecksniff and Micawber, but a much richer and fuller creation than either of those products of Dickens's idealism. The circle of snobbery, however, moves a long way outside Mr. Dorrit and his atrocious children Fanny and Edward, who are similarly worsened by their good fortune. It touches the financier and swindler Merdle, who has selected a wife, not for his own pleasure, but to achieve social position ; and Mrs. Merdle, who has sold her extensive but unfeeling bosom, ideal for the display of jewels, purely upon its snob value (" The bosom moving in Society with the jewels displayed upon it, attracted general admiration "). Even the amiable Mr. and Mrs. Meagles allow their daughter to marry the worthless Gowan because of his distant relation to the Barnacle family. The twin peaks of the book are the points at which the contemptible nature of this snobbery is revealed : the first when Mr. Dorrit admits at a large dinner-party that he was formerly a convict, and the second when Merdle's enterprises collapse and he commits suicide. The central figure in the story, Arthur Clennam, is a grey shadow of the early Dickensian heroes ; he is permitted to achieve happiness after losing all his money in Merdle's swindling concerns and serving a term of purgatory in the Marshalsea.

The same remorseless but hopeless radicalism is at work in *A Tale of Two Cities*. The world of the chocolate-drinking Monseigneur is doomed : but it will be replaced by a tyranny of the people no less vicious than the tyranny of Monseigneur. The use of symbolism in the book is simple but effective ; and, like the symbolism of fog and decay as in *Bleak House*, it comes near the beginning of the book, to mark the fact that it is a key to the tale. A cask of wine has been dropped, and broken, in the street. It lies in little pools among the stones, and people kneel down with scooped hands to drink it, or dip mugs of mutilated earthenware in the puddles, or lick the sodden, lee-dyed pieces of the cask. The wine is drunk up, and some mud with it ; but not before a man has scrawled upon a wall with a finger dipped in wine-lees the word BLOOD. The aristocracy is to be bathed in this blood (in a later chapter the sunset, striking into the travelling carriage of Monsieur the Marquis, steeps its occupant in crimson) : but the defeat of the aristocracy means merely the triumph of " the mob." Between these two evil principles the defeated radical was able to pose no third force, which would triumph by the power of its morality. Sydney Carton's sacrifice is important only in a personal sense ; it stays the wheel of history for hardly more than a second.

There is a sense in which most of Dickens's later works are a rewriting of the earlier ones, from the standpoint of a disillusioned instead of an optimistic radical. *A Tale of Two Cities* is in many respects a maturer *Barnaby Rudge* ; and *Great Expectations*, his next novel, contains much of *David Copperfield* and something of *Nicholas Nickleby*. It is, like them, a picaresque tale of adventure, in which the hero is transparently Dickens himself : but where Nicholas revolts against the savagery of Dotheboys Hall, accepts hardship and discomfort cheerfully, and is perfectly at home in the company of travelling players, Pip reacts to sudden riches like Mr. Dorrit, by ignoring his old friends ; where David Copperfield is granted at least the formal satisfaction of becoming a famous author and making a happy marriage, Pip has cruelly revealed to him the disreputable social basis upon which his well-being is founded and at the end (as Dickens originally wrote it, before he was pressed into a conventional happy ending) has finally lost hope of Estella. Mr. Shaw has remarked of this book that " its beginning is unhappy ; its middle is unhappy ; and the conventional happy ending is an outrage on it." The key passages in

Great Expectations are in those wonderfully clear visual scenes at the beginning when Pip, on Christmas Eve, runs out to take pork pie, cheese, mincemeat and brandy to the convict shivering on the Marshes. Christmas was in the early novels a time celebrated by Dickens with almost intolerable joviality ; it is not accidental that in this story Christmas is associated only with fear, and that Pip finds it a laborious task to stir the pudding for an hour, before going out to his terrible meeting with the convict who kept as a companion a young man who had " a secret way pecooliar to himself, of getting at a boy, and at his heart, and at his liver."

It is not accidental, either, that the opening chapter of Dickens's last completed novel, *Our Mutual Friend*, deals with the robbing of dead bodies, or that the book's plot is concerned with the fortune that has been placed, literally, in a dustheap, and with its effect upon the inheritors. Dickens seems to be saying, in these last books, that all money is tainted ; but on the positive side he can suggest no way of life which is independent of the evils of money. His destructive criticism of this snobbery-ridden, money-worshipping society, however, has now reached the peak of its caricatural power. Some of the masks in this terrifying gallery of lunatic Philistines, hypocrites and toadies are recognisably his friends (Maria Winter becomes Flora Finching, John Forster becomes the overbearing and pompous Podsnap) ; all have been made from the obsessions of a disappointed genius. The Veneerings, a family struggling to establish themselves socially through sheer weight of money, are the chief target in *Our Mutual Friend*. Our first sight of them, and of the guests they entertain to dinner, is done with a hysterical loving hatred, a passionate visual power : Dickens shows each of these masks distorted as they sit under the new Veneering crest (discovered by the College of Heralds) in the dining-room : Podsnap " prosperously feeding," red beads on his forehead, shirt-collar crumpled ; Mrs. Podsnap, " quantities of bone, neck and nostrils like a rocking-horse " ; old Lady Tippins " with an immense obtuse drab oblong face, like a face in a tablespoon, and a dyed Long Walk up the top of her head, as a convenient public approach to the bunch of false hair behind, pleased to patronise Mrs. Veneering opposite, who is pleased to be patronised." The Veneerings them-selves are as nearly as possible blanks—they exist merely as maggots trying to work their way up the decaying social structure. But it is not only the class structure which is seen, at this point, to show the iridescence of decay ; *society itself* has become a symbol of decay in this last book. We are introduced to the place where the Hexams live with the remark that it has " a look of decomposition " ; the first thing Silas Wegg notices when he goes to see his friend Mr. Venus, the " articulator of human bones," is " a pretty little dead bird lying on the counter, with its head dropping on one side against the rim of Mr. Venus's saucer, and a long stiff wire piercing its breast." Images of death and decay recur constantly throughout the book, and it is in these that *Our Mutual Friend* has power and interest ; the successful Jonsonian humours of the early work have become very mechanical, in the persons of Venus and Wegg, the hero and heroine are among their author's weakest creations, and the eccentric good characters like the dolls' dressmaker, Jenny Wren, are nearer than ever to the borders of lunacy. (" I'm often so pressed for time ! I had a doll married, last week, and was obliged to work all night. . . . They take no care of their clothes, and they never keep to the same fashions a month. I work for a doll with three daughters.")

These changes in Dickens's writing are not to be explained simply in terms of a failure in radical belief. His radicalism, as we have seen, was a personal faith, not very far removed from the mania that produced in other unbalanced minds of the period the idea that they possessed the gift of tongues, or that they had been sent into the world with a divine mission to cleanse it of corruption. The radical faith was valuable to Dickens as an artist because it enabled him to keep some kind of grip on external events ; after he had lost it his mind was at the mercy of every cruel wind that touched his quivering sensibility—a disastrous meeting with Maria Beadnell, a casual but wounding remark by a friend. These last books of Dickens's are the work of an author who has increased his power of portraying the visual world in its minutest detail, but is slowly losing his sense of reality. Life, we are continually crying out as we read these painful and wonderful stories, life is not like this ; people are not like this ; these flashes of lightning illuminate nothing but the room of distorting mirrors in which Dickens lived. The characters in his last novels bear the same relation to those in the early work that a gargoyle by an artist of genius bears to a comic cartoon by a draughtsman with a good sense of line. They come from the mind of a man defeated, a man possessed.

Dickens realised the fact, although he did not understand the reason, of his increasing isolation from the world of reality. From the first he attempted to compensate for the wildness of his imagination by exactness in visual description, with results which achieved the effect of caricature through their unnatural minuteness. In an indifferent story written near the end of his life, *George Silverman's Explanation*, he set down his own impression of the film that obscured his view of the world :

" I seem to myself, on looking back to this time of my life, to have been always in the peaceful shade. I can see others in the sunlight . . . but I myself am always in the shadow looking on. Not unsympathetically,—God forbid ! —but looking on alone."

In the last months of his life, Dickens received a letter from a young man working on a provincial newspaper, who asked him the prospect of earning a living by writing. In his reply, the most famous author of his age advised his correspondent on no account to enter literary life in London. " Such an attempt," he wrote, " must lead to the bitterest disappointment."

The Master of Sentiment

The sentiment of Dickens, unlike his radicalism, showed little change through his career. From the melancholy figure of Smike, drooping his way miserably through *Nicholas Nickleby* to a foreseen and happy death, through a long list of ill-treated and dying children, idiots and apprentices—Little Nell and the Marchioness, Barnaby Rudge and Tom Pinch, little Paul Dombey, the " old-fashioned " child, putting already the question that Dickens himself posed a few years later (" Papa, what's money . . . I mean what is money after all ? I mean, papa, what can it do ? "), David Copperfield and Little Jo and Amy Dorrit and Jenny Wren —the sentiment and the figures are unvarying. The catalogue is a tedious one for a modern reader, and the death-bed scenes are more nearly comic than touching :

> He put his hands together, as he had been used to do at his prayers. He did not remove his arms to do it ; but they saw him fold them so, behind her neck.

'Mama is like you, Floy. I know her by the face ! But tell them that the print upon the stairs is not divine enough. The light about the head is shining on me as I go ! '

The golden ripple on the wall came back again, and nothing else stirred in the room. The old, old fashion ! The fashion that came in with out first garments, and will last unchanged until our race has run its course, and the wide firmament is rolled up like a scroll. The old, old fashion— Death !

Oh thank God, all who see it, for that older fashion yet, of Immortality ! And look upon us, angels of young children, with regards not quite estranged, when the swift river bears us to the ocean.

That is the death of Paul Dombey. Such sentimentality was one of the conventions of the Victorian novel, as the worship of violence is a convention of our own time ; it should be accepted or rejected in that light, rather than treated as an exquisite joke or a demonstration of our superior taste. There are good rational reasons for rejecting this Victorian convention of beauty in suffering—its untruthfulness to life and its unconscious use as a cover for Victorian child labour are two of them—without calling into count the fashionable quality of " taste." Dickens's unfortunates exist often in the most wretched conditions, but their virtue cleanses the filthy rags they wear, and purifies the foul air of their surroundings. They are never lice-ridden or pock-marked, or repulsive rather than pitiable ; for their creator knew, or felt in himself, the exact degree and kind of misery that would move his audience. He apprehended perfectly in his own sensibilities the guilt and embarrassment of the Victorian bourgeois when faced with man's inhumanity to man. This writer who slapped his thigh in ecstasy when he brought off a good comic touch and was moved to tears by his own pathos knew, nevertheless, exactly how far a reformer might go in depicting cruelty and suffering to a Victorian audience. This knowledge led him often to perpetrate artistic untruths by his own standards, and at other times to destroy the effect of his pathos with touches of comedy. It is impossible for a modern reader to take seriously the terrors of Dotheboys Hall, when they are described in this manner :

> Mrs. Squeers stood at one of the desks, presiding over an immense basin of brimstone and treacle, of which delicious compound she administered a large instalment to each boy in succession : using for the purpose a common wooden spoon, which might have been originally manufactured for some gigantic pot, and which widened every young gentleman's mouth considerably :. they being all obliged, under heavy corporal penalties, to take in the whole of the bowl at a gasp. In another corner, huddled together for companionship, were the little boys who had arrived on the preceding night. . . . At no great distance from these was seated the juvenile son and heir of Mr. Squeers—a striking likeness of his father—kicking, with great vigour, under the hands of Smike, who was fitting upon him a pair of new boots that bore a most suspicious resemblance to those which the least of the little boys had worn on the journey down—as the little boy himself seemed to think, for he was regarding the appropriation with a look of most rueful amazement.

" Delicious compound," " heavy corporal penalties," " juvenile son and heir," " a look of most rueful amazement "—these are comic phrases, rather reminiscent of Billy Bunter and Greyfriars School ; and it is not surprising that this scene (like that in which Oliver Twist asks for more) has for a long while been much favoured for performance by schoolboy dramatic societies, who play it as uproarious farce. For the Victorians, however, the comedy provided a welcome relief from the picture of cruelty which, unalloyed, would have exacerbated too sharply their sensibilities. Dickens's characters, as Forster remarks,

were "never for a moment alien to either the sympathies
or the understandings of any class"; though it should be
added that their particular appeal was to the Victorian
bourgeoisie.

The range of Dickens's sentiment covered also most
institutions and occasions recognised by the Victorian
bourgeoisie as symbolic pillars of its civilisation : the family
and Christmas are two obvious examples. There are fewer
happy families in the later books than in the early ones, and
there is less concentration upon Christmas festivity ; but
the sanctity of the family and the joy of Christmas were,
nevertheless, themes in which he found continual inspiration.
He wrote a Christmas story each year for the paper he was
editing, although none of the later tales had the success or
the spontaneity of the early *Christmas Carol* ("It seems to
me a national benefit," Thackeray remarked), or *The Chimes*.
It is notable that the later tales which he wrote for *Household
Words* celebrate less the gaiety of the season than its pathos.
"What Christmas is as we Grow Older," published in 1851,
expresses his increasing preoccupation with the sorrows of
the past, his consciousness of missing the perfect marriage
and the perfect friend :

> What ! Did that Christmas never really come when we and
> the priceless pearl who was our young choice were received,
> after the happiest of totally impossible marriages, by the united
> families previously at daggers-drawn on our account. . . . Is
> our life here, at the best, so constituted that, pausing as we
> advance at such a noticeable milestone in the track as this great
> birthday, we look back on the things that never were, as
> naturally and full as gravely as on the things that have been
> and are gone ?

We must accept the ghosts of the past, Dickens tells us, and
remember them.

There was a dear girl—almost a woman—never to be one—
who made a mourning Christmas in a house of joy, and went
her trackless way to the silent City. . . . O look upon her
beauty, her security, her changeless youth, her happiness.

Dickens was writing wholly for himself when he put down
such passages: it is a mark of his singular relationship
with his audience that his references to personal sorrows
were as warmly received as his earlier records of happy
Christmases spent at Dingley Dell or in the company of
Bob Cratchit.

It is in his attitude towards the idea of progress that
Dickens exemplifies perfectly the self-contradictory standpoint of the Victorian bourgeoisie, and the sharp limitations
of his own morality. This attitude may be defined as an
unquestioning acceptance of the fact and tendency of the
Industrial Revolution, combined with a condemnation of its
necessary inhumanity and a continual desire to hark back to
the days before mechanisation. Thus, Dickens was no
Morrisian artist, calling for a return to handicrafts—he
had, in fact, some contempt for the Pre-Raphaelites; and
it never occurred to him that any perils were inherent in
the idea of mass production. Although he accepted the
fruits of scientific progress, however, Dickens was illogically
appalled by their origin, and subordinate manifestations.
This kind of self-deceiving sentiment commonly goes
unremarked by those who exclaim most loudly over the
deaths of Little Nell and Paul Dombey. It is well illustrated
by his glimpse of Coketown and its machinery in *Hard
Times* (a similar glimpse of a manufacturing town is offered
us in *The Old Curiosity Shop*). There is in Coketown red
brick dirtied to an unnatural colour by smoke and ashes,
and interminable serpents of smoke coil out of tall chimneys;
the canal is black, and the river is purple with dye, the

windows in the buildings rattle all day long, while " the piston of the steam-engine worked monotonously up and down, like the head of an elephant in a state of melancholy madness." The picture is a gloomy one—but something is lacking in it ; and that is the moral comment which Dickens makes so readily on any social abuse that really moves his interest. What has he to say about the people of Coketown ? They are, he tells us, very like one another, and they go in and out at the same hours upon the same pavements to do the same work. Then comes the moral comment, and it is surprisingly mild :

> These attributes of Coketown were in the main inseparable from the work by which it was sustained ; against them were to be set off, comforts of life which found their way all over the world, and elegancies of life which made, we will not ask how much of the fine lady, who could scarcely bear to hear the place mentioned.

And that is Dickens's only moral comment upon the existence of such a place as Coketown : within a paragraph or two he has turned to the much more congenial task of castigating Mr. Gradgrind and Mr. Bounderby for bedevilling the lives of Coketown's inhabitants with their utilitarianism. The job of examining the morality of the civilisation that flowered in Coketown was one which Dickens was, in fact, not equipped to undertake ; he lacked the necessary interest in scientific discoveries, and his uneasy social position in the bourgeoisie made it almost impossible for him to attack achievements which were the props of their power. He preferred, whenever his story allowed him reasonably to do so, to avoid such modern issues altogether by placing his tale some twenty or thirty years back in time, in a period when the stagecoach was the recognised means of locomotion.

Dickens's attitude towards the stagecoach and the railway illuminates quite remarkably his dislike (which was never made explicit, because of the contradiction inherent in the idea of a radical looking back wistfully to the days of the stagecoach) for the age of the machine. In *Sketches by Boz* there are three notes on stagecoaches and horse-omnibuses, which are described in affectionate terms, while the very last piece in the book is a " Familiar Epistle from a Parent to a Child aged Two Years and Two Months," recording a journey from Manchester to London by Mail Train. The disconsolate appearance of the guard is noted, " surveying the engine with a look of combined affliction and disgust which no words can describe." The " Parent " whimsically considers the future time " when mail-coach guards shall no longer be judges of horse-flesh—when a mail-coach guard shall never even have seen a horse—when stations shall have superseded stables, and corn shall have given place to coke," and it is plain that the writer's own adherence, like that of the guard, is given to the coach.

The stagecoach is, of course, one of the most important elements in the gaiety of *Pickwick Papers*, and it appears agreeably in *Nicholas Nickleby*. The coach symbolised for Dickens an eccentricity and rich individualism which he missed in the mechanical railway ; and it represented an aspect of feudalism with which he had much sympathy ; but it is likely also that he was drawn to it in recollection of his own childhood. Certain patterns of houses and landscape are repeated again and again in Dickens's work, and these patterns plainly have their origin in an adult vision of childhood much more intense and vivid than is normal. It was in a stagecoach that he had come to London at the age of eleven packed " like game, carriage paid," and he repeated the journey many times in fiction, just as he dealt over and over again with Camden Town and the other parts of North London which he explored in childhood. Later on he pictured repeatedly in decaying houses the tumbledown place on the river at Hungerford Stairs where he spent painful months in the blacking warehouse.

The railway had no place in such a vision of the past, and we should not be surprised, therefore, to find Mr. Weller, senior, complaining in one of the sketches between stories in Dickens's first periodical, *Master Humphrey's Clock*, that "The rail is unconstitootional and an inwaser o' priwileges," and the engine "a nasty, weezin', creakin', gaspin', puffin', bustin' monster, always out o' breath." These observations are made humorously, but later the railway becomes upon occasion a symbol of evil and disaster. When Mr. Dombey goes on a railway journey with Major Bagstock after the death of his son, the occasion is used for stressing in a passage of several hundred words that "The power that forced itself upon its iron way—its own—defiant of all paths and roads, piercing through the heart of every obstacle, and dragging living creatures of all classes, ages, and degrees behind it, was a type of the triumphant monster, Death." Near the end of the book a railway engine, a giant with two red eyes, is the agent that destroys the villainous Carker. It "spun him round and round, and struck him limb from limb, and licked his stream of life up with its fiery heat, and cast his mutilated fragments in the air." In later books, David Copperfield repeats some of his creator's stagecoach experiences, and the remarkable chase undertaken by Bucket and Esther Summerson in *Bleak House* is carried on in "a phaeton or barouche," but in *Hard Times* the railway train ("Fire and steam, and smoke, and red light, a hiss; a crash, a bell, and a shriek ") is an appropriate agent for Louisa's terrified flight from her husband and from Harthouse. After *Hard Times* the railway almost disappears from Dickens's novels ; obsessed with the need to re-create the life of his childhood, he abandons the modern Victorian world. *Little Dorrit* and *Great Expectations* are placed in a period when conditions were those of Dickens's childhood, *A Tale of Two Cities* in the eighteenth century, *Edwin Drood* in Cloisterham (Rochester), " a city of another and a bygone time." *Our Mutual Friend* is set in the present day, " though concerning the exact year there is no need to be precise," but this is a formality for the sake of the Veneerings ; in all essential respects this story, too, might well take place in the early nineteenth century. The only other serious treatment of the railway is in *Mugby Junction*, a Christmas story written in 1866. The story is a poor one, but there is a passage which shows the thoughts that seem to have sprung naturally to Dickens's mind on sight of a railway train. A typical late Dickensian traveller (" a man within five years of fifty either way, who had turned grey too soon . . . a man with many indications on him of having been much alone ") stands on Mugby Junction platform, and sees a railway train pass in the gloom " which was no other than the train of a life," a life bearing a strong resemblance to what Dickens at the age of fifty-four imagined his own life to have been :

> Here mournfully went by a child who had never had a childhood or known a parent, inseparable from a youth with a bitter sense of his namelessness, coupled to a man the enforced business of whose best years had been distasteful and oppressive, linked to an ungrateful friend, dragging after him a woman once beloved. Attendant, with many a clank and wrench, were lumbering cares, dark meditations, huge dim disappointments, monotonous years, a long jarring line of the discords of a solitary and unhappy existence.

The anti-mechanical and feudal spirit which is represented by this contrast between the virtuous stagecoach and the wicked railway corresponded to an emotional need in Dickens ; but it is important to notice that it corresponded, also, to the emotional requirements of his public. Dickens's relation to his public, as a novelist and later in his public readings, was a series of love affairs in which he met with very few repulses. On the rare occasions when Dickens miscalculated public reaction to his writings he became very worried ; if the miscalculation was a serious one he abandoned, or made radical changes in, his original conception. An early instance of a successful interpretation of his public's need is that of *Pickwick Papers*, which was not strikingly successful until the appearance of Sam Weller ; once this note had been struck, in the sixth number, Dickens deliberately altered the shape of his picaresque adventure to make Sam Weller its real hero. The particular note here was that of the faithful but not servile retainer, the comically impertinent member of the lower classes who yet knows his place upon any important occasion, the independent and intelligent Cockney who acknowledges the amiable and stupid Pickwick as his master. " Sam Weller introduces the English people," says G. K. Chesterton in what is surely the most curious tribute paid to this Dickensian character, " Sam Weller is the great symbol in English literature of the populace peculiar to England." Sam Weller, it may more truly be said, is a figure out of feudal England brought not too closely up to date. He is a triumph of comic sentiment ; not until he created Little Nell did Dickens sound the note of pathos with equal success.

It is instructive to look also at one of Dickens's failures, to see how he was able to mould his own taste when necessary to conform to that of his public. In 1839 he proposed to edit and write a new weekly publication which should be issued at the price of threepence. It was to relate the history of a little club of characters ; to contain anecdotes of Mr. Pickwick and Sam Weller ; to include amusing essays and references to current events ; to embody a series of papers containing stories and descriptions of London, divided into portions like the *Arabian Nights* and called " The Relaxations of Gog and Magog," and another series—" something between *Gulliver's Travels* and the *Citizen of the World*"—which would satirise the administration of justice ; and a record of a visit by the editor to either Ireland or America " introducing local tales, traditions and legends." This sufficiently ambitious scheme matured, after the usual meditations about a title, as *Master Humphrey's Clock*. Master Humphrey, an odd but lovable figure, was to extract manuscripts from the bottom of his " old, cheerful, companionable clock," on the themes already specified.

For once, Dickens had seriously misjudged the feeling of his audience—and it is noteworthy that almost the only occasions on which he did so were those on which he attempted to speak to them directly in his own person, rather than through the medium of fiction. The first number of the periodical sold nearly 70,000 copies, but orders dropped away as soon as the readers discovered that there was no continuous tale. Dickens's reaction was simply to give his readers what they wanted. He abandoned the grandiose plans for conversations between Gog and Magog, and almost all the rest of his programme as well ; instead, he expanded a " little tale " for which several titles were canvassed, including *Master Humphrey's Narrative* and *A Passage in Master Humphrey's Life* into the immensely successful full-length story, *The Old Curiosity Shop*.

The full realisation of his ability to touch the Victorian heart with pathos (for Oliver Twist and Smike, who had preceded Little Nell, were half-length drawings lacking the absolute purity and unworldliness that were essential elements in her success) set Dickens on a path from which he never wavered. Comic and pathetic sentimental characters may be found in almost every one of his books ; and as his foot never wavered, so his touch never faltered in creating them.

This perfect union of writer and public allowed Dickens to project again and again in such characters the fantasies embodied in his recollections of Maria Beadnell and Mary Hogarth ; and his insistence on such fantasies ordered his attitude towards sex. In Dickens, as in that other great Victorian novelist, George Eliot, we can discover two figures—a successful writer who conformed to the standards and conventions of the period (and even, in certain respects, helped to embed those conventions in national life by their books), and a literary artist of great power and originality who managed sometimes, almost unconsciously, to subvert those conventions. This dichotomy of unconscious artistic aim and conscious commercial effect, had its basis in the popular movements towards political radicalism, feminine emancipation and social reform upon one hand, and in the strictness of Victorian morality and the crudeness of Victorian optimism on the other : and in no writer is the dichotomy more marked than in Dickens. He was inclined by nature, as we can discover from his correspondence, to be fairly frank in sexual matters ; but the iron hoops of convention held him firmly—and indeed, they were rarely irksome, for as we have seen they corresponded very much to his needs as a respectable Victorian. Within these hoops he produced such contemporary triumphs of pathetic sentiment as Little Nell and Jenny Wren, and of comic sentiment as Sam Weller and Mark Tapley. But sometimes Dickens tried to burst the hoops, sometimes he was aware that saccharine ran instead of blood in the veins of these conceptions ; and then he put down figures whose sexuality is not less plain because it is repressed.

Several of these figures are sadists. In the early books they are pictured half-jokingly ; Mr. Squeers is a comic sadist, and the element of comedy is still very marked in the wife-tormentor Quilp (whose activities do nothing to reduce his wife's affection) ; but Mr. Murdstone, Mr. Creakle and Rosa Dartle in *David Copperfield* are three different kinds of sadist, all put down quite seriously, and acting as a balance to the childish charm of Dora. Mr. Murdstone, David's stepfather, is a tyrant who beats and persecutes the child in the name of religion and character-building ; Mr. Creakle takes a delight in beating the boys in his charge ; Rosa Dartle is a more complicated figure, who has been turned into a sadist through her love for Steerforth, who burned and disfigured her by accident in his boyhood. Dickens uses symbols to express the cruelty of Mr. Murdstone and his sister which, like almost all his symbols, are more effective than direct statement. When David first learns that Mr. Murdstone has married his mother, he wanders down into the yard and there finds the empty dog-kennel " filled up with a great dog—deep-mouthed and black-haired like Him," who " sprang out to get at me." The incident prefigures very well the treatment he is to receive from Mr. Murdstone ; as the impact of Miss Murdstone upon the shrinking David is immediately and subtly made through description of " her two un-compromising hard black boxes, with her initials on the lids in hard brass nails " ; and her hard steel purse, kept

" in a very jail of a bag which hung upon her arm by a heavy chain, and shut up like a bite." There are undertones here which are more terrifying than any obvious account of cruelty could be ; and there are undertones, too, in the portrait of Mr. Creakle, who speaks always in a whisper, and who " had a delight in cutting at the boys, which was like the satisfaction of a craving appetite."

The most notable of these portraits, however, is that of the disfigured Rosa Dartle. When Rosa learns that Emily has run away with Steerforth, her desire for love is released in an outburst of passionate hatred :

> They (the Peggottys) are a depraved, worthless set. I would have her whipped ! . . . I would have his house pulled down. I would have her branded on the face, drest in rags, and cast out in the streets to starve. If I had the power to sit in judgment on her, I would see it done. See it done ? I would do it ! I detest her. If I ever could reproach her with her infamous condition, I would go anywhere to do so. If I could hunt her to the grave, I would. If there was any word of comfort that would be a solace to her in her dying hour, and only I possessed it, I wouldn't part with it for life itself.

Such hints of sexual perversity may be found in all of the later novels, hidden usually behind the mask of respectable Victorian " oddness." Hortense, Lady Dedlock's French maid in *Bleak House*, for example, is enraged when the young and pretty new maid is allowed to place a shawl on her mistress's shoulders, and to ride away in her carriage. In retaliation—the touch is one which, in its irrational appropriateness, shows Dickens's uncanny awareness of the right kind of apparent irrelevance—Hortense takes off her shoes and walks deliberately after the carriage, through thick, wet grass. Miss Wade, in *Little Dorrit*, who hates all men and has delusions of persecution, lures away the sultry good-looking girl servant Tattycoram from her home with the Meagles, and makes her into an inseparable companion. Mr. Edmund Wilson, in a note on Miss Wade, comments on the " remarkable pre-Freudian insight " with which Dickens gives a case-history of a woman who has the delusion that she can never be loved. Mr. Wilson appears to miss the point that there is a reasonable explanation for Miss Wade's conduct : that she is a Lesbian. That solution, of course, cannot be advanced by Dickens, and in the " History of a Self-Tormentor " through which Miss Wade explains her conduct, she is saddled with an unhappy love affair. Her curious delusions of persecution, however, date further back, for we learn that in early girlhood she loved " in a passionate way " a girl who was her " chosen friend." Miss Wade was jealous of all her friend's acquaintances. " When we were left alone in our bedroom at night, I would reproach her with my perfect knowledge of her baseness ; and then she would cry and cry and say I was cruel, and then I would hold her in my arms till morning." Such descriptions reveal the urgent need Dickens felt to describe sexual relations in some other terms than those demanded by his public.

There is an attempt to fulfil this need, also, in the line of cruelty that runs through many of his attempts to portray the emotional relations of men and women. This can be seen in Steerforth's behaviour to Little Em'ly and, reversed, in her behaviour towards David (" She liked me but she laughed at me and tormented me ") ; it is very evident in Quilp's attitude to his wife, and—reversed again—in Estella's cruelty to Pip. Such cruelty is a necessary complement to Dickens's sentimentality. Across the figures of Little Nell, the Marchioness and Jenny Wren fall the menacing shadows of Quilp and Mr. Murdstone. The last books show a decrease both of sentimentality and of cruelty ; they had been transferred to the public readings in which the absurdities of Toots made the audiences weep with pleasant joy, and Sikes's brutality to Nancy made them faint.

THE SENSE OF HORROR AND THE SENSE OF HUMOUR

Dickens's taste for the horrific has already been noted; but it extended far beyond the interest in hangings and mob violence apparent in the historical novels. The apparatus he used for the early horror stories contained in *Pickwick Papers* was derived from the Gothic novel, although the imagery in such tales as " A Madman's Manuscript " was peculiarly Dickensian. It is possible that, later, he may have been influenced by Edgar Allan Poe, whose stories he read and enjoyed on his first trip to America. But Dickens's truest creations of horror—the terrible ride taken by Jonas Chuzzlewit and Montague Tigg, the heavy air of doom that hangs about Lady Dedlock's " place " in Lincolnshire, the atmosphere of the Marshes in *Great Expectations*—are all linked with scenes and objects much more than with people.

Dickens had an extraordinary feeling for houses, and for weather. He devotes a great deal of space to describing houses almost from the start of his writing, and frequently uses them as one of the keys to the nature of a story or a character. I do not think there is a single long novel, after *Pickwick Papers*, in which Dickens fails to describe at length a wretched and ramshackle house, set usually in an urban landscape. Jacob's Island, in *Oliver Twist*, gives a foretaste of these scenes of desolation. The visitor there, Dickens says :

> Walks beneath tottering house-fronts projecting over the pavement, dismantled walls that seem to totter as he passes,

chimneys half crushed, half hesitating to fall, windows guarded by rusty iron bars that time and dirt have almost eaten away, every imaginable sign of desolation and neglect. . . .

(A stranger) will see the inhabitants of the houses on either side lowering from their back doors and windows, buckets, pails, domestic utensils of all kinds, in which to haul the water up ; and when his eye is turned from these operations to the houses themselves, his utmost astonishment will be excited by the scene before him. Crazy wooden galleries common to the backs of half-a-dozen houses, with holes from which to look upon the scene beneath ; windows, broken and patched, with poles thrust out, on which to dry the linen that is never there ; rooms so small, so filthy, so confined, that the air would seem too tainted even for the dirt and squalor which they shelter ; wooden chambers thrusting themselves out above the mud, and threatening to fall into it—as some have done ; dirt-besmeared walls and decaying foundations ; every repulsive lineament of poverty, every loathsome indication of filth, rot, and garbage ; all these ornament the banks of Folly Ditch.

Dickens always uses such scenes as background for the fate and situation of his characters. In this case the description acts as prelude to Sikes's attempt to escape his pursuers by dropping into Folly Ditch. Thus also the " small rat-infested dreary yard call ' Quilp's Wharf,' " with its fragments of rusty anchors and piles of rotten wood, is a suitable place for the hunchback's machinations, and the decayed aspect of Mr. Haredale's house in *Barnaby Rudge* at once symbolises the passing of feudalism and prefigures the burning of the house near the end of the story. Such symbolism is no doubt often unconscious ; but in the later books at least it is frequently used with more conscious intention. The desolation of the Dedlocks' " place " in Lincolnshire in *Bleak House* has already been noted : but the tone of the book is found on the first page in the fog that refers not only to the Court proceedings in Jarndyce *v*. Jarndyce, but to the fates of the characters :

> Fog everywhere. Fog up the river, where it flows among green aits and meadows ; fog down the river, where it rolls defiled among the tons of shipping, and the waterside pollution of a great (and dirty) city. Fog on the Essex marshes, fog on the Kentish heights. Fog creeping into the cabooses of collier-brigs, fog lying out on the yards, and hovering in the rigging of great ships ; fog drooping on the gunwales of barges and small boats. Fog in the eyes and throats of ancient Greenwich pensioners, wheezing by the firesides of their wards ; fog in the stem and bowl of the afternoon pipe of the wrathful skipper, down in his close cabin ; fog cruelly pinching the toes and fingers of his shivering little 'prentice boy on deck.

The weather is rarely fine in the later Dickens ; and even when the sun shines the warmth it gives is not kindly, as it was to Mr. Pickwick or Nicholas Nickleby. The " blazing sun upon a fierce August day " on the first page of *Little Dorrit* has the effect of making the eyes ache and the parched trees droop. It is, we are told, like a white-hot arrow ; it oppresses equally horses and their recumbent drivers and the exhausted labourers in the fields. Dickens's view of life in his later years was such that no kind of weather appeared benevolent to him, neither the sun of Marseilles which shines oppressively in the first chapter of *Little Dorrit*, nor the Sunday evening, " gloomy, close and stale " that greets Arthur Clennam when he returned to England. Church bells now are " maddening . . . of all degrees of dissonance," where once they would have sounded sweetly. The holy quiet of the Sabbath—as it might have been called in the earlier stories—has changed into a vision of despair. " Nothing to see but streets, streets, streets. Nothing to breathe but streets, streets, streets. Nothing to change the brooding mind, or raise it up. Nothing for the spent toiler to do, but to compare the monotony of his seventh day with the monotony of his six days." Clennam returns to a typical piece of late-Dickensian architecture, propped precariously on " some half-dozen gigantic crutches." This house collapses suddenly at the end of the book, burying the criminal Blandois : " It heaved, surged outward, opened asunder in fifty places, collapsed, and fell. . . . The great pile of chimneys which was then alone left standing, like a tower in a whirlwind, rocked, broke and hailed itself down upon the heap of ruin, as if every tumbling fragment were intent on burying the crushed wretch deeper."

Dickens achieved his horrific effects—and, as we shall see, his humorous ones, too—by sheer weight of description, combined with the use of the verbal equivalent of a slow-motion cinematic technique. He is one of the few English novelists whose descriptions really do gather power as they increase in length. The fog in *Bleak House* is at first, for the reader, a mere fog : but as Dickens extends it to envelop visual object after object, and then, with a neat twist, turns it to include also the High Court of Chancery—and not only the physical reality of the Court but the abstract idea of it as well—as all this takes place, the fog becomes an unforgettable image fixed in the reader's mind. The terrifying characters in Dickens often disturb the imagination more by the force of the conditions in which they are placed than by their actions. Dickens's method of characterisation is unlike that of any other writer in English. He catches first, generally, the scene—a decaying house, a rat-infested yard, the stuffed interior of a taxidermist's shop, a room in which every clock has stopped at twenty minutes to nine ; and within that framework a puppet enacts over and over again with lunatic fervour a

single activity. Quilp capers and batters and shrieks like a
demonic Punch, Mr. Venus broods over his stuffed treasures
and articulated bones, Miss Havisham dreams of past hopes
of happiness in her bridal dress. There is a sense in which
all Dickens's important characters are conceived as Jonsonian
humours, marking some comic or gruesome aberration of
the human personality : but if this is a limitation, in the
sense that we see little more of Major Bagstock than his
laugh or of Uriah Heep than his humility, it is responsible
also for the extraordinary depth Dickens is able to give to
his figures. His conscious power of observation, clearly,
was limited to externals : but he was able to describe those
externals with such passion that his characters take on a
reality quite other than that generally obtained by realistic
representation.

This peculiarity of characterisation makes Dickens's
horrific characters at times uncommonly like his humorous
ones. The activities of Quilp and Wackford Squeers are
always threatening, as we have seen, to turn into comedy ;
and there is, on the other hand, something very gruesome
about the Fat Boy in *Pickwick Papers*, whose leaden eyes
twinkle between mountainous cheeks. Leering horribly
upon the food which he unpacks from a basket, the Fat Boy
acts in typical Dickensian slow motion. " The fat boy rose,
opened his eyes, swallowed the huge piece of pie he had
been in the act of masticating when he last fell asleep, and
slowly obeyed his master's orders—gloating languidly over
the remains of the feast, as he removed the plates, and
deposited them in the hamper." The fat boy is a little too
obviously a case of glandular trouble for a twentieth-century
reader to be quite comfortable in his company.

An interesting article published several years ago in *The
London Hospital Gazette* written by the late Lord Brain

observes solemnly that the Fat Boy is " surely the first recorded case of narcolepsy associated with obesity," and discusses Dickens's remarkably accurate clinical descriptions of nervous disorders, shown in the symptoms attributed to Mrs. Joe Gargery after her attack by Orlick, the cerebral arteriosclerosis of the Honourable Mrs. Skewton in *Dombey and Son*, the symptomatic epilepsy of Anthony Chuzzlewit, the hypomania of the lunatic who makes advances to Mrs. Nickleby, and the psychiatric eccentricities of the Small-weeds, Miss Havisham, and Mr. Dick. We have no means of knowing where Dickens gained his medical knowledge, but it is notable that the symptoms described by him correspond almost exactly in many instances to features of his own behaviour. Anthony Chuzzlewit's attack is similar to Dickens's " spasms," Mrs. Gargery and the Honourable Mrs. Skewton suffer from the jargon aphasia to which Dickens in his later years was often subject, the lunatic in *Nicholas Nickleby* talks nonsense remarkably similar to that talked by Dickens upon occasion. It is likely, at least, that he drew upon his own experience when he turned these pathological cases, and many others, into savage comedy.

There is a popular idea that all of Dickens's books overflow with humour ; and it is true that he had a " humorous eye," so that everything he wrote turned into humour, or at least into a kind of jocosity that sometimes has an unintentionally gruesome effect. But even a cursory examination of his humour shows that it worked on at least three levels, two of them quite alien to the professional humourists who regard Dickens as their exemplar. There is, first, riotous farce ; second, the humorous treatment of pathological figures ; third, the biting humour linked to his criticism of society. These three kinds of humour had each its relation to Dickens's own character : the first to his overwhelming high spirits, the second to the fascination natural freaks held for him, the third to his sensitiveness about his social position. In *Pickwick Papers* we are given farce upon a plane which was never reached again by Dickens, and has not been touched at all by any other English novelist. The book begins, like the *Sketches by Boz*, with the Jonsonian fooling of dupes (a detailed comparison of Dickens with Jonson would reveal the immeasurable damage that Victorian society did to the emotional truth of its artists). The Pickwickians are so foolish that they are almost feeble-minded. They are at the mercy of any rogue, like Jingle, who makes himself moderately amiable to them ; they discover, and gloat over, an antiquarian treasure which consists of a stone with letters inscribed on it which read : " ⊦ BILST UM PSHI S.M. ARK " ; innocence leads them to involvement in ridiculous duels and equally ridiculous love affairs. There is nothing remarkable in these adventures, sired by Jonson out of Surtees : but they are carried on with such extraordinary high spirits and such power of external observation that the reader is overwhelmed into accepting a world of fantasy on its own terms. The world of farce is not usually a fantastic one ; the point in the farcical behaviour of most fictional characters—the thing that makes them exquisitely risible—is their *nearness* to the world of social convention which they conscientiously flout. This side of Dickens's comedy, however, is as nearly as possible pure fantasy. Mr. Jingle talks like a madman, Dr. Slammer behaves like one and so does Payne (the man with the camp stool) ; there is none of the background of ordinary human living which provides the flavour of most farcical comedy. This world of fantasy, however, was one in which Dickens could live himself ; it was the world in which he danced a hornpipe dressed as a sailor outside

Catherine Hogarth's house, or professed insane love for Queen Victoria ; or in which he slid from his chair to the floor at a dinner-party, when a woman called her husband " darling," and lay on his back waving a leg and crying, " Did she call him darling ? " It is probably true to say that he described no exaggeration in any of his characters which he could not imagine in himself.

The world of *Pickwick's* first chapters was almost too strange for its audience ; the book did not become really acceptable until the sentimental comedy of Sam Weller had been introduced, and Mr. Pickwick and his friends pulled into something nearer human shape. In his writings, as in his life, Dickens never lost altogether this feeling for fantastic comedy, but it was much reduced and adulterated. We meet it in the conversation of Mrs. Nickleby—taken, we are told, from that of Dickens's mother, but we can be sure that it was not taken literally ; in the " single gentleman " who booked lodgings for two years in Sampson Brass's house and then " pulled down the window-blinds, drew the curtains, wound up his watch, and, quite leisurely and methodically, got into bed " to sleep for twenty-six hours ; in Major Bagstock, who laughs like a maniac and always refers to himself in the third person ; in Mr. Dick ; in Maggy, the woman in *Little Dorrit* who believes herself to be ten years old. But with time and disillusionment there is a recognisable change in the nature of the fantasy in these figures (and there are dozens more who could be mentioned with them) ; they are more obviously pathological, and generally less amiable. The high spirits change perceptibly into queer spirits ; the world of the early *Pickwick* was a world Dickens never regained.

His more important comic characters take on, instead, many resemblances to human beings, and are used for pointing morals about human behaviour. The qualities of Mrs. Gamp and Pecksniff are exaggerated, to be sure, but many of their traits are precisely those we encounter in our acquaintances ; Mrs. Gamp personifies Greed and Pecksniff Hypocrisy. Slowly these hard colours turn to subtler ones, to characters who, although they are still essentially no more than one facet of a personality magnified and distorted, are seen with sympathy and understanding. Pecksniff, Micawber and old Dorrit show the same portrait worked out three times, with increasing subtlety. Pecksniff is a Jonsonian humour, mechanical in conception but brought to oily life by his creator's bursting energy. Micawber is Pecksniff made amiable ; all of his actions are viewed as delightful whimsicalities although many of them are susceptible to the interpretation of hypocrisy placed by Dickens on everything done by Pecksniff. Finally Pecksniff and Micawber are combined in old Dorrit, that mixture of pompous snobbery and pathetic ineptness firmly fixed in the third period of Dickens's humour—the period in which it is linked inseparably with his social criticism. It is particularly in this third period that almost every character in the stories (except the hero and heroine, and the figures of pathetic sentiment) may be called humorous. The humour has now come to exist as something independent of the stories' morality ; it runs over into the behaviour of almost every character. No doubt Dickens meant the end of the swindling Mr. Merdle to provide a moral lesson ; yet what can be more essentially *comic* than the description of him " suddenly getting up, as if he had been waiting in the interval for his legs, and they had just come " ; or of Miss Havisham saying to Pip, " I have a sick fancy that I want to see some play. There, there ! " with an impatient movement of the fingers of her right hand, " Play, play,

play " ; or the description of Mrs. Veneering's aristocratic appearance : " Each of her eight aquiline fingers looking so very like her one aquiline nose that the bran-new jewels on them seemed necessary for distinction's sake. . . . Mrs. Veneering, in a pervadingly aquiline state of figure, and with transparent little knobs on her temper, like the little transparent knobs on the bridge of her nose." But the comedy has become so bitter, so firmly joined to Dickens's consciousness of personal defeat, to his hatred of the upper class and of those who, like the Veneerings, betray their own class by trying to move out of it, that in a Pickwickian sense it is no longer comedy at all.

CHAPTER III

THE ARTIST

THE art of a novelist is the matrix that shapes his view of reality. For some writers this matrix changes with the years ; for others it exists, as a mould into which the free flow of ideas may be poured, from the moment they begin to write. A writer whose talent is rich, disordered and violent—a writer, in fact, like Dickens—is fortunate if he lives in a period when literary conventions are strict, so that a matrix is provided ready-made for his ideas. It was Dickens's misfortune that he did not live in such a period ; that he began to write, instead, at a time when the English novel was changing from a picaresque romance to a plotted narrative, and from a record of events to an analysis of character. Dickens lived through this time of change, and was aware of it ; and we see in his books the struggles of a creative artist who lacked a form in which to set down his apprehension of the world. The task of constructing such a form was one for which Dickens was not fitted, although he heroically attempted it. The form he did create—the particular Dickensian method by which his novels were put together—was a ramshackle one ; it could never hold the weight of his writing or the richness of his characterisation : it is one reason for the flawed view of reality that we get from his work.

When he began to write Dickens was concerned simply to produce a story suitable for publication in monthly numbers—one, that is to say, in which each instalment should have its small climax and its meed of excitement :

the *Pickwick Papers* are in effect an eighteenth-century picaresque tale, with a dash or two of Gothic horror added. There is no evidence that Dickens disliked the need to write for monthly part publication. Like other Victorian novelists, he accepted it quite willingly, and it made his work, like theirs, frequently prolix and verbose. Such a method of work suited very well the needs of one who positively enjoyed working at a great speed, and for long periods at a time ; but it hampered Dickens as an artist. Very probably he did not think of himself in that light : but he soon became conscious of the need to impose some kind of shape on his stories. The kind of middle-class characters with whom he was, at first, most at home, did not fit easily into a rambling tale : the record of their ambitions and defeats, and of the cruelties they suffered at the hands of an unjust social order, demanded a carefully constructed and fairly rigid plot. These characters (people, it may be said with a touch of over-simplification, like Dickens himself) had to be treated seriously ; their fates roused Dickens's deepest feelings about the aspiring bourgeoisie. He tried to provide a suitable plot for their activities in his second novel, *Oliver Twist* ; and in all of the novels after the end of what is sometimes called the " first period " of his work with *Martin Chuzzlewit* care and rigidity in construction became for him a main concern. In this movement towards " plot " he showed remarkable originality, for most of his contemporaries at this time still relied upon some variant of historical or picaresque romance ; but Dickens's inability at first to handle the form he wished to use is shown by the pile of coincidence on which *Oliver Twist* is built. Dame Una Pope-Hennessy, in her life of Dickens, has recounted in detail three of the most outrageous coincidences in the book : that when

Oliver runs away to London he is drawn into the power of Fagin, who by chance happens to be an ally of Oliver's stepbrother ; that Oliver attempts to pick the pocket of, and is adopted by, a man who was his grandfather's best friend ; and that when Oliver is forced by Bill Sikes to become a burglar, he enters the house in which lives his mother's sister, Rose. But at the same time that we notice the incredibilities upon which the story is based, we observe also that these coincidences are remarkably well concealed.

For such concealment Dickens uses from the first tricks which resemble remarkably those of the modern detective-story writer. He presents characters whose relation to each other is apparently inexplicably strange ; the reader's curiosity is roused by this strangeness, and he reads the book partly with the object of solving a problem. In *Oliver Twist*, for example, we are not told for a long time that Monks, Oliver's stepbrother, is an ally of Fagin ; instead, we are introduced to Monks as a dark, mysterious figure who for some reasons of his own wishes Oliver to be made into a " sneaking, snivelling pickpocket." Such a procedure is typical. In *Oliver Twist* it creates only con-fusion, because of the clumsy mechanism of interlocking coincidences ; but in *Great Expectations* the trick is used with absolute mastery, to induce the reader's belief that Pip's fortune comes from Miss Havisham instead of from the convict Magwitch. This device of concealment is used in other books, and Dickens has almost as good a title as Edgar Allan Poe to be called the father of the detective story. (" Inspector Bucket of the Detective," the human bloodhound of *Bleak House*, is probably the most vividly presented fictional detective before Sherlock Holmes.) This creation of a puzzle as a focal point of interest was Dickens's special contribution to the form of the novel. He was not, however, like the modern detective-story writer—or like his young friend Wilkie Collins—interested in the puzzle for its own sake. It was to him simply a convenient medium for conveying the melodrama which chiefly concerned him. The plot was always a nuisance to Dickens, although it was a nuisance that held for him a continual and increasing fascination. In reading *Edwin Drood*, indeed, one is impressed equally by the weariness with which Dickens handles the characters and the remarkably firm grasp he retains upon the plot. The puzzle framework, used always rather uneasily, alternates with the adventure story as the form in which his work is cast. *Bleak House* and *Our Mutual Friend* are built round a puzzle ; *David Copperfield* and *Great Expectations* are stories of adventure, although the puzzle enters as an element into *Great Expectations*. Within these forms—forms which had to be worked out with the strictest care—Dickens placed the figures of his world : his set pieces of sentiment like Little Nell and Paul Dombey, his patterns of uninteresting virtue and their complementary patterns of interesting vice—and behind them the gallery of grotesques that is unparalleled in our literature.

Dickens's conscious view of reality is contained in the melodramatic interaction of these set figures on the framework of a puzzle. The bourgeois hero, timidly active, feebly good, horrified by violence, moves like a puppet in the shadow of two sets of loathsome figures : the criminals who would like to destroy the values of bourgeois society altogether, and the aristocrats who express contempt for it. Both criminals and aristocrats are wicked Fagin and Sir Mulberry Hawk, Dennis and Sir John Chester, Madame Defarge and Monseigneur : they are all attempting to rape the innocent body of the bourgeoisie, from which true virtue comes. The criminal element pursues the bourgeois hero with unfailing malignity—although sometimes the malignity is craftily disguised as benevolence, as in the case of the convict Magwitch who tries to corrupt Pip with riches which are tainted by their source, even though they have been honestly earned. The aristocracy works differently. Behind a pretence of unconcern it attempts to crush the spirit of the bourgeoisie through such mediums as the Circumlocution Office or the Court of Chancery. The professional classes, with very few exceptions, are the lackeys of the aristocracy ; and the aristocracy governs the country, offering to the intelligent bourgeoisie the chimera of choice between Buffy, Cuffy and Duffy and Boodle, Coodle and Doodle. And the people of England watch warily this struggle between the virtuous bourgeoisie and the wicked criminals and aristocrats. Who are the people of England, the watchers on the sidelines ? Sam Weller and Mr. Dick ; Newman Noggs and Vincent Crummles ; Tom Pinch and Wemmick. The eccentrics, the failures, the feeble-minded, the valets and the strolling actors—these Dickensian representatives of the English people lend at least tacit support to the bourgeoisie in their struggle with the forces of evil. But in the last novels, although the characterisation has not changed, the novelist has lost faith in his own virtuous figures. Is the struggle, he wonders, a genuine one—is virtue really inherent in the bourgeoisie as a class ? Does money make its bourgeois possessor of necessity respectable and well-intentioned ? At the end even that shibboleth has been questioned.

That, substantially, is the view of reality consciously presented by Dickens : a view which, obviously, we find unacceptable to-day. Here it is necessary to make a distinction between the interest inherent for us in Dickens's viewpoint, and the interest we feel in discovering his reasons for holding it. The latter interest is behind much recent criticism of Dickens, from Hugh Kingsmill's alert but supercilious view of him in *The Sentimental Journey*, to Mr. Edmund Wilson's fascinating interpretation of Dickens's personality in his long essay " The Two Scrooges." Such an interpretation as Mr. Wilson's is immensely valuable in helping us to understand the subconscious motives that move beneath Dickens's work. The early part of this book is an excursion from Mr. Wilson's sentence, one of the few illuminations in the morass of Dickensian criticism :

> The work of Dickens' whole career was an attempt to digest (his) early shocks and hardships, to explain them to himself, to justify himself in relation to them, to give an intelligible and tolerable picture of a world in which such things could occur.

It has been remarked already that to understand Dickens's work one must understand his peculiar psychological make-up : but such an understanding is not a substitute for literary criticism. There are no absolute standards for evaluing works of literature : a critic can do no more, when he is assessing the work of an artist who pretends to deal directly with the world of living men and women, than compare the artist's overt view of reality with the nature of reality itself. It is when we make this test that the flaws in Dickens's view of reality are apparent. His works reflect life with an extraordinary intensity, but they reflect it in a distorting mirror. As an artist Dickens was a victim of the Philistinism, the prudery and the sentimentality of his age : although through the peculiar power of the artist to act as a reagent in his society, he was partly responsible through his own work for the Victorian qualities that damaged his art.

C.D.—6

There is a phrase in Mr. Wilson's essay in which he suggests that the artist with whom Dickens has most in common is Dostoievsky. No sooner has the comparison been made (Mr. Wilson does not follow it up) than its justice is realised ; but it is a terribly damaging one to Dickens. We find in Dostoievsky an artist, hopelessly neurotic and unbalanced and occupied like Dickens with the psychology of crime and punishment, who yet managed to produce a picture of mankind's attitude to religion, politics and love which has presented unexpected, and unwanted, truths to later generations. We find in Dickens an artist who, in general, conformed to the deadly conventions in literature demanded by his class ; who rejected the uncomfortable truths about the social and sexual life of man which his class did not wish to hear. It is, no doubt, significant that Dostoievsky suffered in fact the torments that Dickens felt chiefly in imagination : that he spent years in a Siberian prison camp and not months in a blacking warehouse, that he was an ostracised and penniless gambler convinced of man's essential virtue and beauty instead of a successful author with an obscure sensation of personal loneliness. From his years of suffering and poverty Dostoievsky gave us a Raskolnikov for a Bill Sikes, an Alyosha for a Little Nell, a Verhovensky for a Madame Defarge. The comparison between Dostoievsky and Dickens shows us the vast landscapes of the soul which Dickens never knew, the terrible corridors of the spirit down which this respectable member of the Victorian bourgeoisie never walked.

These are hard words : does anyone doubt that they are true ones, outside the closed circle of admirers who venerate Dickens, like Doctor Johnson, as an English institution ? Is it not plain that there is a dreadful falsity in Dickens's celebrated pathetic creations which makes them altogether unacceptable as pictures of human beings—a falsity made more shocking by the fact that upon these half-human figures the artist spent most prodigally his astonishing talent ? A principle is involved here which is much more than a difference of taste between one age and another : that something more, in fact, which is precisely the artist's obligation to put down fully and clearly, as he sees them, the features of reality. It is true that the Victorians were able to accept these characters (although even among the Victorians there were dissentients) : but, quite certainly, they could not have been accepted, or expressed, in any other age. The Victorian intelligentsia was subject to quite peculiar strains and stresses, and hampered by inhibitions unique in English literary history ; such inhibitions, such stresses, made them susceptible to pathos which revolts the spirit in its untruth. It is impossible for us, as it would have been impossible for an Augustan or an Elizabethan, to view without disgust these abortions of the spirit : just as we are bound to feel distaste for Dickens's approval of the masochistic adoration which David Copperfield feels in the presence of Steerforth or Pip in the presence of Estella. In the whole of Dickens's work there is not one relationship between a man and a woman which is adult, rather than a product of childish fantasy. This is not a matter simply of the limitation of Victorian convention about the relations of men and women. That, certainly, was hampering enough ; but George Eliot (in *Middlemarch* and *Daniel Deronda*) and Trollope (in half a dozen of his late novels) showed that it was not an insuperable obstacle. The causes of Dickens's failure were partly technical, in that the form he had chosen was adapted for melodrama, which does not permit the subtle treatment of character ; but behind the technical limitation is a deep defect of the spirit.

So much must be said in dispraise of Dickens : everyone under forty who reads Dickens to-day must have felt much of what is said here, although few care openly to express it. If, then, the plots of Dickens's work are ingeniously devised to lend mystery to melodrama ; and if his material is treated with the loud superficiality which is characteristic of the melodramatist : what is it that gives these tales of blood and saccharine such an urgent, compelling and terrifying power ? What makes certain scenes in almost any book by Dickens more memorable than anything written by Trollope, George Eliot, or indeed any other English novelist ? What is the indestructible residue in Dickens's art that holds us absorbedly attentive, and makes us pull through much that in any other author would impel instant rejection ? What, in fact, has Dickens to offer a modern reader ?

He offers, first, an unparalleled visual sense, a capacity which never fails in setting down memorably the features of a human being, a house or a landscape. This vision is not a literal one ; it comes from the fantasy world of childhood in which lies the seed of all Dickens's works. His apprehension of the external world in its physical aspects, however, is not blurred by adherence to Victorian convention : the distorting mirror held up to nature reflects back to us from the first splendid, comic and horrible images in turn. Here is Solomon Pell, the attorney, a very minor character in *Pickwick Papers* :

> Mr. Solomon Pell . . . was a fat flabby pale man, in a surtout which looked green one minute and brown the next : with a velvet collar of the same cameleon tints. His forehead was narrow, his face wide, his head large, and his nose all on one side, as if Nature, indignant with the propensities she observed in him in his birth, had given it an angry tweak which it had never recovered.

We see Mr. Pell with remarkable clarity, and yet we hardly see him as a human being. There is, in fact, too much description of Mr. Pell, and it is too remarkable, for us to be able to assimilate his literal appearance into a world in which appearances and colours are altogether more commonplace than they are in the books of Dickens. The cameleon surtout and the nose on one side are effects of imagination, not of literal portraiture. Such effects are heightened in Dickens's maturity, when the figure is linked inseparably with its surroundings. Mr. Vholes, Richard Carstone's " legal adviser " in *Bleak House*, is first introduced to us as " a sallow man with pinched lips that looked as if they were cold, a red eruption here and there upon his face, tall and thin, about fifty years of age, high-shouldered and stooping. Dressed in black, black-gloved and buttoned to the chin, there was nothing so remarkable in him as a lifeless manner, and a slow fixed way he had of looking at Richard." This is adequate enough : but we learn much more of Mr. Vholes when, a few pages later, his office is created with the pathological exactness and excess of detail found in surrealist painting :

> Mr. Vholes's office, in disposition retiring and in situation retired, is squeezed up in a corner, and blinks at a dead wall, Three feet of knotty floored dark passage brings the client to Mr. Vholes's jet black door, in an angle profoundly dark on the brightest midsummer morning, and encumbered by a black bulk-head of cellarage staircase, against which belated civilians generally strike their brows. Mr. Vholes's chambers are on so small a scale, that one clerk can open the door without getting off his stool, while the other who elbows him at the same desk has equal facilities for poking the fire. A smell as of unwholesome sheep, blending with the smell of must and dust, is referable to the nightly (and often daily) consumption of mutton fat in candles, and to the fretting of parchment forms and skins in greasy drawers. The atmosphere

is otherwise stale and close. The place was last painted or whitewashed beyond the memory of man, and the two chimneys smoke, and there is a loose outer surface of soot everywhere, and the dull cracked windows in their heavy frames have but one piece of character in them, which is a determination to be always dirty and always shut, unless coerced.

Such a passage is the result, at first glance, of photographically exact observation : but is produced in reality by an extraordinary sensibility to the physical world. One might suggest that the author of such a passage suffered from a mild claustrophobia, and that his senses of smell and colour were abnormally developed : but, in fact, Dickens was quiveringly sensitive to *every* facet of external reality. It is safe to say that every chapter of every one of his books contains some description in which a heightened reality is achieved through a heightened sensibility. Very often the effect is obtained by the illusion of photography already mentioned ; sometimes one seems to be looking at a still from an expressionist film. Miss Havisham's room in *Great Expectations*, which has been left untouched for years as a constant reminder of the betrayal she suffered upon her wedding-day, can be conceived most easily as a set for *The Cabinet of Dr. Caligari* :

From that room . . . the daylight was completely excluded, and it had an airless smell that was oppressive. A fire had been lately kindled in the damp, old-fashioned grate, and it was more disposed to go out than to burn up, and the reluctant smoke which hung in the room seemed colder than the clearer air—like our own marsh mist. Certain wintry branches of candles on the high chimney-piece faintly lighted the chamber : or, it would be more expressive to say, faintly troubled its darkness. It was spacious, and I daresay had once been handsome, but every discernible thing in it was covered with dust and mould, and dropping to pieces. The most prominent object was a long table with a tablecloth spread on it, as if a feast had been in preparation when the house and the clock all stopped together. An epergne or centre-piece of some kind was in the middle of this cloth ; it was so heavily overhung with cobwebs that its form was quite undistinguishable ; and, as I looked along the yellow expanse out of which I remember its seeming to grow, like a black fungus, I saw speckled-legged spiders with blotchy bodies running home to it, and running out from it, as if some circumstance of the greatest public importance had just transpired in the spider community.

I heard the mice too, rattling behind the panels, as if the same occurrence were important to their interests. But the black beetles took no notice of the agitation. . . .

The oddity of Wemmick's house in the same book—a wooden cottage with a Gothic door and windows, a flagstaff (" on Sundays I run up a real flag "), a drawbridge which crosses a moat four feet wide, and a gun, protected by a tarpaulin umbrella, which is fired at nine o'clock every night—is similarly enhanced by the straight-forward way in which it is described. Dickens employs the method of surrealist painting, by describing the fantastic shapes and figures that occupy his mind in the soberest tones of naturalism : but there is an important difference between his attitude and that of the surrealists. Dickens worked without self-consciousness, in the belief that he was using the real colours of everyday life ; the surrealists are highly self-conscious artists, well aware of their own quaintness and queerness. The strangeness of Dickens is natural ; that of the surrealists is, however ingeniously, contrived. One should be careful, when saying that Dickens's characters are grotesque, to emphasise that they were not grotesques for him, but truthful projections of his intensely felt imaginative life.

Dickens's subconscious view of reality (as distinct from the conscious view which he propounded through the morality of his elaborately plotted coincidence-filled melo-dramas) is conveyed generally through this use of naturalist description to enhance the effect of material which is essentially pathological. At the same time his naturalism, curiously, rendered acceptable to the Victorian public characters who, like Miss Havisham or Mr. Dick, might otherwise have been dismissed as lunatics ; or, like his gallery of predatory lawyers, as caricatures so wild as to be ludicrous. But so considerable is the power of this artist that he makes us accept the actions of his lunatics as tragic or comic studies in character ; and his legal caricatures achieve a profundity altogether denied to Trollope's varied and uniformly skilful attempts to present lawyers as reasonable human beings.

Dickens's work, indeed, derives part of its power from his apparent deficiencies. He is careful to avoid any attempt to describe the workings of the Circumlocution Office or the Court of Chancery ; and it is probable that he was temperamentally incapable of understanding them, just as he was incapable of understanding the practical operation of Parliament. But by this very vagueness and evasiveness Dickens is able to turn these institutions into social fables ; and his portraits of members of the pro-fessional classes, similarly, gain much of their effectiveness from the fact that such people were for Dickens slightly unreal. To a child a schoolmaster, a policeman, a lawyer, are figures removed from ordinary living ; and Dickens regarded them very much as a child might have done. In comparing Dickens's lawyers with Trollope's, one notices that Trollope is immensely concerned to convince the reader that a member of the legal profession is a man like anybody else : whereas Dickens makes it plain that they are a species apart from ordinary humanity. And yet it is the Dickensian lawyers and barristers that we remember individually, where Trollope's merge into one vast archetypal figure. Trollope's lawyers have a literal, Dickens's an imaginative and fabulous, truth.

Dickens's characteristic method of achieving the intensity which many have praised and few analysed is, then, the accumulation of detail. Phrase is added to phrase to build up a personality with, very often, one key phrase that brings the figure startlingly before us, like the observation that Mr. Vholes had " a red eruption here and there upon his face." The red eruption is so much at variance with the rest of the picture—a thin, sallow, high-shouldered stooping man in black—that it fixes Mr. Vholes for us permanently. The figure thus created is placed in its appropriate setting, and then acts in accordance with the suggestions offered by its appearance and habitat. Mr. Vholes, thus, is clearly a vulture ready to prey upon the body of young Richard Carstone ; and his reappearance in the story to bring bad news of Richard is marked by the repetition of the key phrase through which we bear him in mind. " Mr. Vholes . . . secretly picked at one of the red pimples on his yellow face with his black glove."

We cannot afford to skip a line or a phrase of these descriptions if we wish fully to apprehend the skill of Dickens's characterisation. But although he works generally by addition and repetition, he can set down an appearance, when he wishes to do so, in one powerful visual or verbal image. What more do we need to know of Mr. Chadband than that he is " a large yellow man, with a fat smile, and a general appearance of having a good deal of train oil in his system," who " moves softly and cumbrously, not unlike a bear who has been taught to walk upright " ? How clearly we see the unimportant character, Lady Tippins :

" Charming old Lady Tippins " with " a certain yellow play
in (her) throat, like the legs of scratching poultry." And
what a remarkable creation is the old woman in *Little Dorrit*
who has no other name than Mr. F.'s Aunt :

> An amazing little old woman, with a face like a staring
> doll too cheap for expression, and a still yellow wig perched
> unevenly on the top of her head, as if the child who owned
> the doll had driven a tack through it anywhere, so that it only
> got fastened on. Another remarkable thing in this little old
> woman was, that the same child seemed to have damaged her
> face in two or three places with some blunt instrument in the
> nature of a spoon ; her countenance, and particularly the tip
> of her nose, presenting the phenomena of several dints, generally
> answering to the bowl of that article.

The activities of these figures, and their dozens of relations
in Dickens's books, represent for us what is valuable in his
work. These products of an injured child's imagination are
symbols as well as characters, and they exist not in the
world of literal reality, but " on the perpetually shifting
frontier between ordinary life and the terror that would
seem to be more real." The common ground between
Dickens and the surrealists has already been suggested ; and
the phrase quoted above from Kafka's notebooks suggests
another writer whose work resembles in many ways that
of Dickens. Kafka, too, obtains effects through the
accumulation of detail ; he is capable of the same distortion
through the illusion of photographic exactness ; he shows
the same over-developed sensibility to external stimuli ; his
figures are much more important as symbols than as literal
characters ; like Dickens, Kafka is an insistent moralist.
And the final merit of Dickens's work, like that of Kafka,
is that through the distortions and the morality there is
conveyed to us a social fable. The fable, in the case of

Kafka, touches the whole nature of man as a social and religious animal ; in the case of Dickens, it deals with man's relation to Victorian society.

Dickens is the greatest creative writer of the Victorian age in England ; his work is its chief ornament, and his life its saddest literary catastrophe. It is probable that the effect of his childhood experiences upon his psychological make-up would, in any time, have prevented him from presenting anything like a realistic picture of the world. But the extremest personal pressure applied to a writer may (as in the case of Dostoievsky) still permit him to produce wholly viable work. When the pressure of society, however, is added to the psychological influences which operated in the case of Dickens, they exert a force that can hardly be withstood. Dickens capitulated to Victorian society, and with the whole force of his conscious mind produced the work expected of him ; indeed, one places a modern gloss on an inevitable result, in writing that he " capitulated." Consciously, Dickens desired nothing more than to be the spokesman of the rising Victorian bourgeoisie ; consciously, he felt and expressed their laughter at the " lower orders," their feelings of pathos about children and reverence for the family, their indignation at social injustices which affected themselves : consciously he was, as Hugh Kingsmill remarks, " a true English child of the French Revolution." But he knew this consciously composed picture to be inadequate, because it did not include all the elements of his own nature ; and these elements, expressed in his life by extravagances of speech and action, emerge in his work through the amazing caricatures of people and scenes, which Dickens took for reality.

It follows, then, that Dickens cannot offer us a perfect

novel ; his work is a collection of magnificent fragments, held together by the author's ingenuity, and by his unscrupulous use of coincidence. But his distorted vision reveals, in a way we can never forget, the rotten remnants of feudal society, the inefficiency and corruption of Parliament ; it ridicules the deceits of philanthropy and the formality of law ; it illuminates, above all, the strangest recesses of the human personality. Had he lived in another age, Dickens might have done much more ; or he might, perhaps, not have been a novelist at all, but another kind of artist. But he worked in the Victorian age : his genius was thwarted, but his work was praised. He was in some respects a literary casualty : but there were compensations, in his lifetime, in becoming a national possession.

INDEX

who earned far less than Dickens, found it possible to maintain large families and live comfortably without working themselves to death. Why was Dickens unable to do so ? The answer to that question must be given in psychological, rather than in purely practical terms ; a compulsive desire for continual change and excitement marked the writer whose work in many minds typifies a Victorian settled domesticity and calm.

This compulsion is manifest in his continual travelling, his changes of home, the abrupt notes he sent to friends enjoining them to accompany him on a ride or walk. " Come, come, *come*, and walk in the green lanes. You will work the better for it all the week. COME ! I shall expect you." This note, sent to John Forster, is typical of many others. His visits abroad sometimes extended to months at a time, and when he returned to England he found it difficult to stay in one place for long. He was unable to write until he had reached a pitch of emotional excitement ; once this point had been reached he wrote with great speed and for long periods of time, with very little apparent sign of strain. Whether at work or engaged simply in amusing himself, his energy was always overwhelming. Many friends remarked on his great flow of animal spirits, which found vent in such pranks as a visit to the Hogarths' home, made before he married Catherine, when he appeared outside the window dressed as a sailor and dancing a hornpipe ; or the occasion at Broadstairs, soon after Mary Hogarth's death, when he danced down the jetty with a young woman and held on to a tall upright pole at the end of it while the water splashed round their knees and she screamed, " My dress ! my only silk dress ! " ; or his extraordinary conduct at the time of Queen Victoria's marriage, when he did no work for days, wrote of " raving with love for the Queen," said that he loathed his parents, detested his house and was irritated by his wife, and wrote to the mystified Landor of "running away to some uninhabited island with a maid of honour, to be entrapped by conspiracy for that purpose." These animal spirits overflowed into dozens of interests and activities. He concerned himself with rehousing and sanitary reform ; he investigated in person and then denounced in novels the administration of workhouses and the level of education in private schools ; he retained a lifelong interest in the reformation of prisons. His interest in prisons, in hanging, and in criminal mentality and habits, was, indeed, extra-ordinary. It appears in novel after novel, and was not less evident in his life. While in Paris he went frequently to the Morgue, until he was so repelled by something he saw that for a long time he lacked courage to go back ; *American Notes* contains elaborate and lengthy comparisons of American prisons with English ones: he attended, and afterwards fervently condemned, several executions. Dickens's conscious interest in these facets of life was exerted purely from a humanitarian viewpoint. He wrote letters to the Press protesting against capital punishment and public executions, and pleading for more humane prison conditions ; but, as Mr. Edmund Wilson has remarked, there is also a subconscious pathological interest, through which Dickens identifies himself with the criminal, or at least shows a sympathy for criminal activities which is quite outside the range of feeling that might be expected as a result of his father's imprisonment. There is no indication that Dickens ever felt that justice had not been done to his father ; his identification of himself in some degree with criminals grew from the sense of inferiority based on his unhappy childhood experience at the blacking warehouse.

His success as a writer was great and dramatic, but it was never sufficient to wipe out the painful memories of childhood and youth, and in his books he relives again and again, with endless variations, the situations of that period. They had a reality for him which was increased, rather than dissipated, by their evocation in fiction.

In his daily life Dickens was a strong partisan of the need for educational and social reform. He was favourably impressed in 1840 with the demand for a People's Charter ; but he had no faith that reforms would be effected through Parliament, and he never for an instant regarded himself as a political revolutionary. Mr. Shaw tells a story that when Mazzini called on him Dickens did not know the visitor's name and sent down a guinea to be rid of him. The incident may never have occurred (it seems to be contradicted by some details in Forster's biography), but it has an apocryphal truth, for Dickens viewed reform as something immediate and personal to himself. He was frequently invited to stand for Parliament, but never did so. In his late twenties he gave monetary considerations as the reason for refusal, but in later years he was much more emphatic. Parliament, he remarked in one letter, was "just the dreariest failure and nuisance that ever bothered this much-bothered world," and to another correspondent he wrote : "I have thoroughly satisfied myself . . . that I can be far more usefully and independently employed in my chosen sphere of action than I could hope to be in the House of Commons ; and I believe that no consideration would induce me to become a member of that extraordinary assembly." Dickens believed, or was interested, solely in the prospect of direct reform offered through the approach of individuals to individuals ; and he lent the weight of his words and voice only to socie es which had such short-term practical objects in view. It was with a view to effecting such reforms personally that in 1850 he started the magazine *Household Words*. At one time he thought of calling the paper *Charles Dickens*, and he clung to the idea that to bind the contents together there should be created a " semi-omniscient, omnipresent, intangible creature " called The Shadow. All correspondence was to be addressed to The Shadow, and he was to issue warnings from time to time that he was about to expose humbugs or attack abuses. The Shadow would "loom as a fanciful thing all over London . . . a sort of previously unthought-of Power going about." *Household Words* became a reflector rather than an educator of public taste, and the omnipresent Shadow remained in its editor's mind : but Dickens's part in running this magazine shows very well the power of concentration he could give to any subject, and also his inability to maintain an even flow of interest. The letters that he wrote to his assistant editor, W. H. Wills, show that he scrutinised articles with the utmost care before and after printing, altered tenses, made proof corrections, and did a great deal of work personally which most editors leave to subordinates. The articles that he wrote himself for the paper, most of them ephemeral, were worked on as painfully as masterpieces ; he writes to Wills, characteristically, that he " sat nine hours without stirring " at an article on the Metropolitan Protectives. But these bursts of energy alternated with times when it was difficult for Wills to get replies or decisions from his editor, or when Dickens would go abroad at very short notice and yet expect to see proofs as regularly as if he were in England, or when he would express simply a restless dissatisfaction with the contents of the magazine.

It seems likely that Dickens was vaguely conscious from